NE능률 영어교과서

대한민국 고등학생 **10**명 중 **4.7**명이 보는 교과서

영어 고등 교과서 점유율 1위
(7차, 2007 개정, 2009 개정, 2015 개정)

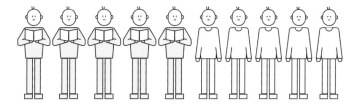

능률보카

그동안 판매된
능률VOCA 1,100만 부

대한민국 박스오피스
**천만명을 넘은 영화
단 28개**

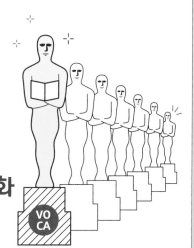

리딩튜터

그동안 판매된
리딩튜터 1,900만 부
차곡차곡 쌓으면 19만 미터

**에베레스트
21 배 높이**

에베레스트 8,848m

190,000m

KB065980

그래머존

그동안 판매된 450만 부의 그래머존을 바닥에 쭉 ~ 깔면
1000km 서울-부산 왕복가능

서울

부산

READING
Inside
STARTER

지은이	NE능률 영어교육연구소
선임연구원	조은영
연구원	이선영, 유소영
영문교열	Curtis Thompson, Angela Lan, Olk Bryce Barrett
디자인	김연주
내지 일러스트	최주석, 박응식, 김동현
맥편집	김재민

NE능률이
미래를
창조합니다.

건강한 배움의 고객가치를 제공하겠다는 꿈을 실현하기 위해
40년이 넘는 시간 동안 열심히 달려왔습니다.

앞으로도 끊임없는 연구와 노력을 통해
당연한 것을 멈추지 않고

고객, 기업, 직원 모두가 함께 성장하는 NE능률이 되겠습니다.

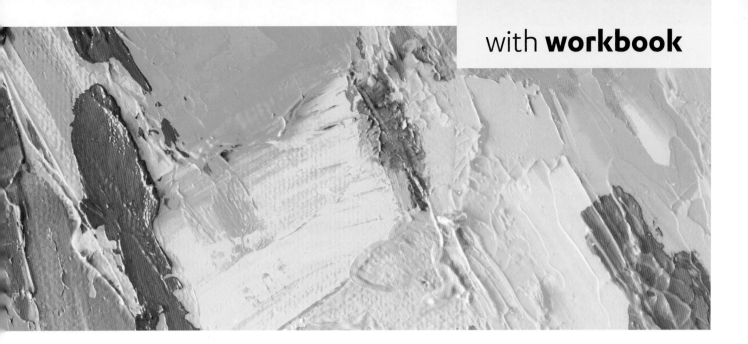

with **workbook**

READING
Inside

STARTER

with **workbook**

STRUCTURES

● This shows how each reading passage is related to the topic and the school subject.

● Reading Comprehension

The students' understanding of the passage is checked through a series of multiple-choice and descriptive questions. This also helps to strengthen students' reading accuracy.

Origin
History

Listen to Your Heart

One day in 1816, a French doctor named René Laennec **went** for a walk. He **saw** two boys playing with a hollow stick. One boy was scraping the stick with a pin while his friend **listened** at the other end. The tube-shaped stick was making the tiny noise very loud!

Months later, Laennec was consulted by a young woman with heart problems. Suddenly, he **remembered** the boys' game. He **rolled** up a piece of paper to make a tube. When he **put** it to her chest, he could _____! He was inspired by this idea, so he **made** a long, wooden tube. This was the first 10 stethoscope.

Afterwards, other stethoscopes were designed. In 1852, George Cammann, a doctor from New York, **made** a metal stethoscope with two earpieces. It **looked** similar to the modern one, and the design has been used ever since. He didn't patent his stethoscope, because he 15 **thought** all doctors should be able to use it for free.

Vocabulary
Check the boxes as you find the words in the passage.

□ go for a walk
□ hollow
□ scrape
□ noise
□ consult
□ inspire
□ metal
□ similar
□ modern
□ for free

Answer Key p. 2 | READING 1

Reading Comprehension

1 What is the best title for the passage?
a. The Stethoscope: How Was It Invented?
b. An Important Discovery about Heart Disease
c. How Stethoscopes Advanced Medical Science
d. René Laennec: The Greatest Doctor in History

2 What is the best choice for the blank?
a. help her feel relaxed
b. cure her heart problems
c. not hear any sound at all
d. hear her heartbeat clearly

3 Write T if the statement is true or F if it's false.
[1] René Laennec made the first stethoscope out of wood. _____
[2] René Laennec's stethoscope looked similar to the modern one. _____

Writing Practice
4 According to the passage, why didn't George Cammann patent his version of the stethoscope?
It's because he thought _____

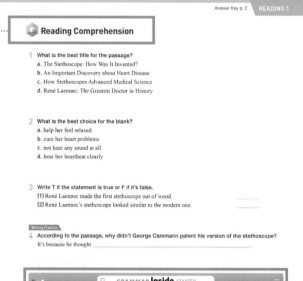

GRAMMAR **Inside** STARTER

일반동사의 과거형 1
• 일반동사의 과거형은 과거에 일어난 일을 나타내며, 주어의 수와 인칭에 관계없이 보통 「동사원형 + -(e)d」의 형태로 쓴다.

Link to...
Chapter 04
Unit 03

listen → listened   move → moved   cry → cried   stop → stopped
• 다음과 같은 불규칙 변화형에 유의한다.

break → broke	buy → bought	come → came	cut → cut	do → did
drink → drank	eat → ate	give → gave	go → went	have → had
make → made	meet → met	put → put	read → read	see → saw
sit → sat	take → took	tell → told	think → thought	write → wrote

Check Up 다음 밑줄 친 단어를 과거형으로 고쳐 쓰시오.
1 I go to bed late. → _____   2 He comes to my house. → _____

Reading Inside Starter | 9

8 | UNIT 01

● Vocabulary

While learners are reading the passage, they can check how many key words they know from the passage. Through this simple activity, they can pick up academic words they didn't know and guess their meanings.

● GRAMMAR **Inside**

This helps learners grasp the key structures of sentences and strengthens their understanding of the passage. It is also related to the best-selling grammar series *Grammar Inside*.

📁 From the **Link to...** , ●

learners can see which chapter and unit of the *Grammar Inside* series are directly related to this section.

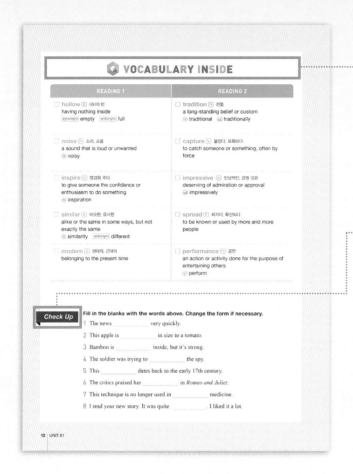

● VOCABULARY INSIDE

This presents content words in context and provides synonyms, antonyms, and related parts of speech to improve students' vocabulary. Learners should check if they know the words first before proceeding with the further learning.

● Through Check Up ,

students can better understand the practical usage of words by filling in the blanks with words from the chart.

Workbook

The workbook, which is composed of four pages of vocabulary tests, grammar tests, and writing tests helps reinforce what students have learned in the main text.

CONTENTS

Link to GRAMMAR **Inside**

	Grammar Points in *Reading Inside Starter*		Grammar Inside Series	
Unit 01	1. 일반동사의 과거형 1	**Starter Ch.04**	Unit 03 일반동사의 과거형 1
	2. 일반동사의 과거형 2	**Starter Ch.04**	Unit 04 일반동사의 과거형 2
Unit 02	1. 감각동사 + 형용사	**Starter Ch.07**	Unit 02 동사의 종류 2
	2. 동사 + 목적어 + 목적격 보어(명사/형용사)	**Starter Ch.07**	Unit 02 동사의 종류 2
Unit 03	1. 수여동사 + 간접목적어 + 직접목적어	**Starter Ch.07**	Unit 01 동사의 종류 1
	2. 동사 + 목적어 + 목적격 보어(to부정사)	**Level 1 Ch.05**	Unit 03 목적격 보어가 필요한 동사
Unit 04	1. 조동사 can	**Starter Ch.08**	Unit 01 can, may
	2. 조동사 must, have/has to	**Starter Ch.08**	Unit 02 must, have to
Unit 05	1. 현재진행형	**Starter Ch.09**	Unit 01 일반동사의 현재진행형 1
	2. 동명사의 역할	**Level 1 Ch.09**	Unit 03 동명사의 역할
Unit 06	1. 대명사 one vs. it	**Level 1 Ch.07**	Unit 02 this, that, it Unit 03 one, some, any
	2. 원급 비교	**Level 1 Ch.08**	Unit 03 원급, 비교급, 최상급
Unit 07	1. 형용사 비교급	**Starter Ch.10**	Unit 01 비교급
	2. 부사 비교급	**Starter Ch.10**	Unit 01 비교급
Unit 08	1. 명사적 용법의 to부정사	**Starter Ch.11**	Unit 01 명사처럼 쓰는 to부정사
	2. 수와 양을 나타내는 형용사 few, little	**Level 1 Ch.08**	Unit 01 형용사
Unit 09	1. 부사적 용법의 to부정사 (목적)	**Starter Ch.11**	Unit 02 형용사, 부사처럼 쓰는 to부정사
	2. 형용사적 용법의 to부정사	**Starter Ch.11**	Unit 02 형용사, 부사처럼 쓰는 to부정사
Unit 10	1. to부정사를 목적어로 취하는 동사	**Starter Ch.11**	Unit 01 명사처럼 쓰는 to부정사
	2. 동명사를 목적어로 취하는 동사	**Level 1 Ch.09**	Unit 03 동명사의 역할
Unit 11	1. 접속사 when, before, after	**Starter Ch.12**	Unit 02 when, before, after, because
	2. 등위접속사 and, but, or	**Starter Ch.12**	Unit 01 and, but, or
Unit 12	1. 접속사 because, if	**Level 1 Ch.11**	Unit 03 because, if, that
	2. 접속사 that	**Level 1 Ch.11**	Unit 03 because, if, that

UNIT 01 | Origins

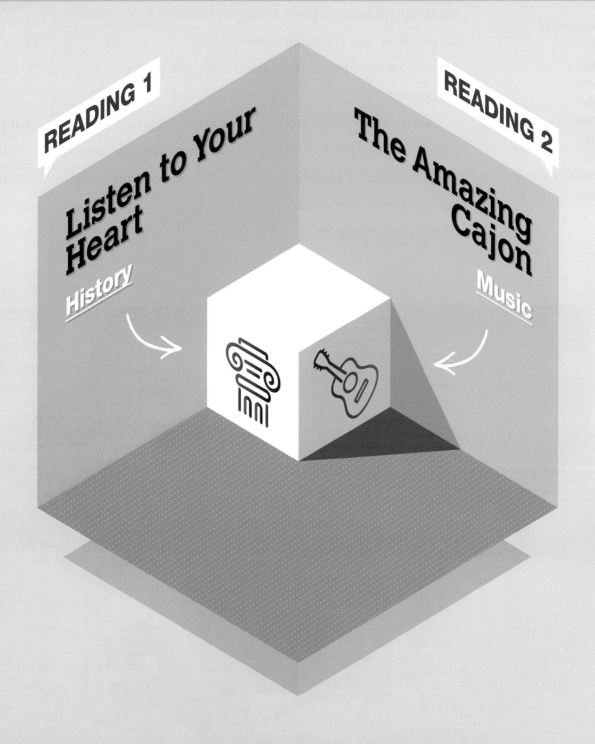

161 words

Listen to Your Heart

One day in 1816, a French doctor named René Laennec **went** for a walk. He **saw** two boys playing with a hollow stick. One boy was scraping the stick with a pin while his friend **listened** at the other end. The tube-shaped stick was making the tiny noise very loud!

Months later, Laennec was consulted by a young woman with heart problems. Suddenly, he **remembered** the boys' game. He **rolled** up a piece of paper to make a tube. When he **put** it to her chest, he could _____! He was inspired by this idea, so he **made** a long, wooden tube. This was the first ₁₀ stethoscope.

Afterwards, other stethoscopes were designed. In 1852, George Cammann, a doctor from New York, **made** a metal stethoscope with two earpieces. It **looked** similar to the modern one, and the design has been used ever since. He didn't patent his stethoscope, because he ₁₅ **thought** all doctors should be able to use it for free.

5

ⓥ Vocabulary

Check the boxes as you find the words in the passage.

☐ go for a walk
☐ hollow
☐ scrape
☐ noise
☐ consult
☐ inspire
☐ metal
☐ similar
☐ modern
☐ for free

Reading Comprehension

1 **What is the best title for the passage?**
   a. The Stethoscope: How Was It Invented?
   b. An Important Discovery about Heart Disease
   c. How Stethoscopes Advanced Medical Science
   d. René Laennec: The Greatest Doctor in History

2 **What is the best choice for the blank?**
   a. help her feel relaxed
   b. cure her heart problems
   c. not hear any sound at all
   d. hear her heartbeat clearly

3 **Write T if the statement is true or F if it's false.**
   (1) René Laennec made the first stethoscope out of wood. _____
   (2) René Laennec's stethoscope looked similar to the modern one. _____

Writing Practice
4 **According to the passage, why didn't George Cammann patent his version of the stethoscope?**
   It's because he thought _____.

GRAMMAR Inside STARTER

일반동사의 과거형 1

• 일반동사의 과거형은 과거에 일어난 일을 나타내며, 주어의 수와 인칭에 관계없이 보통 「동사원형 + -(e)d」의 형태로 쓴다.

    listen → listen**ed**   move → mov**ed**   cry → cr**ied**   st**op** → stop**ped**

Link to ...
   Chapter 04
      Unit 03

• 다음과 같은 불규칙 변화형에 유의한다.

break → **broke**	buy → **bought**	come → **came**	cut → **cut**	do → **did**
drink → **drank**	eat → **ate**	give → **gave**	go → **went**	have → **had**
make → **made**	meet → **met**	put → **put**	read → **read**	see → **saw**
sit → **sat**	take → **took**	tell → **told**	think → **thought**	write → **wrote**

Check Up 다음 밑줄 친 단어를 과거형으로 고쳐 쓰시오.

   1 I go to bed late. → _____   **2** He comes to my house. → _____

The Amazing Cajon

Vocabulary

Check the boxes as you find the words in the passage.

☐ amazing
☐ instrument
☐ tradition
☐ slavery
☐ capture
☐ impressive
☐ spread
☐ nowadays
☐ acoustic
☐ performance

The Peruvian *cajon is an interesting instrument. It looks like a box, and players sit on it and play it with their hands! It looks simple, but it can produce a wide range of musical tones.

The story of the cajon begins in West Africa. West Africa has rich drumming and dancing traditions. (①) During the time of slavery, 5 many West Africans were captured and brought to the Americas. (②) The African slaves in coastal Peru missed their traditional drumming, but they **didn't have** drums anymore. (③) **Did** this **stop** them from drumming? No! (④) The sound was impressive!

This was the birth of the cajon. Later, the cajon became popular 10 among Spanish flamenco players and eventually spread to jazz, blues, and rock. Nowadays, the cajon is used in many kinds of modern music, and it is especially popular for acoustic performances.

*cajon 카혼(직육면체 나무상자 모양의 타악기)

Reading Comprehension

1 **What is the best title for the passage?**
   a. The History of the Cajon
   b. Music Culture in West Africa
   c. How Percussion Instruments Work
   d. Play Your Own Music with a Cajon!

2 **Write T if the statement about the Peruvian cajon is true or F if it's false.**
   (1) It produces a limited range of tones. _____
   (2) It was created by African slaves. _____

3 **Where would the following sentence best fit?**

> They had plenty of old shipping crates, so they decided to play the crates like drums.

   a. ①   b. ②   c. ③   d. ④

Writing Practice

4 **According to the passage, what is the cajon especially popular for nowadays?**
   It is especially popular for _____.

🔍 **GRAMMAR Inside** STARTER   ≡

일반동사의 과거형 2

• 일반동사 과거형의 부정문은 주어의 수와 인칭에 관계없이 「didn't + 동사원형」 형태로 쓴다.

  ..., but they **didn't** *have* drums anymore.
  I **didn't** *go* to work yesterday.

• 일반동사 과거형의 의문문은 주어의 수와 인칭에 관계없이 「Did + 주어 + 동사원형 ~?」 형태로 쓴다.

  A: **Did** this *stop* them from drumming?   B: Yes, it **did**. / No, it **didn't**.
  A: **Did** she *call* you back?   B: Yes, she **did**. / No, she **didn't**.

Link to ...
☐ Chapter 04
☐ Unit 04

Check Up 다음 문장을 주어진 조건에 따라 다시 쓰시오.

  1 I ate pizza yesterday. (부정문으로)   → _____

  2 She read the newspaper. (의문문으로) → _____

◆ VOCABULARY INSIDE

READING 1	READING 2
☐ **hollow** ⓐ (속이) 빈 having nothing inside [synonym] empty [antonym] full	☐ **tradition** ⓝ 전통 a long-standing belief or custom ⓐ traditional ⓐd traditionally
☐ **noise** ⓝ 소리, 소음 a sound that is loud or unwanted ⓐ noisy	☐ **capture** ⓥ 붙잡다, 포획하다 to catch someone or something, often by force
☐ **inspire** ⓥ 영감을 주다 to give someone the confidence or enthusiasm to do something ⓝ inspiration	☐ **impressive** ⓐ 인상적인, 감명 깊은 deserving of admiration or approval ⓐd impressively
☐ **similar** ⓐ 비슷한, 유사한 alike or the same in some ways, but not exactly the same ⓝ similarity [antonym] different	☐ **spread** ⓥ 퍼지다, 확산되다 to be known or used by more and more people
☐ **modern** ⓐ 현대의, 근대의 belonging to the present time	☐ **performance** ⓝ 공연 an action or activity done for the purpose of entertaining others ⓥ perform

Check Up   **Fill in the blanks with the words above. Change the form if necessary.**

1 The news _____ very quickly.

2 This apple is _____ in size to a tomato.

3 Bamboo is _____ inside, but it's strong.

4 The soldier was trying to _____ the spy.

5 This _____ dates back to the early 17th century.

6 The critics praised her _____ in *Romeo and Juliet*.

7 This technique is no longer used in _____ medicine.

8 I read your new story. It was quite _____. I liked it a lot.

UNIT
02 | Economics

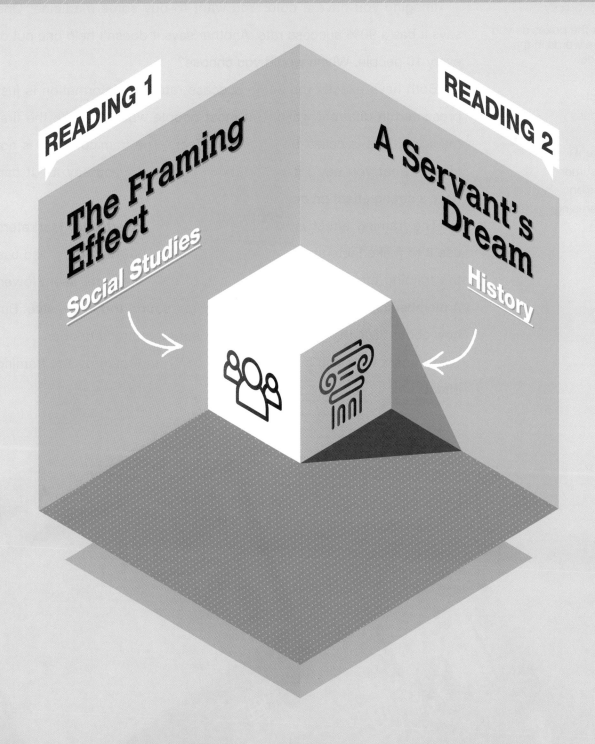

READING 1

The Framing Effect

Social Studies

READING 2

A Servant's Dream

History

Economics

Social Studies

159 words

The Framing Effect

Imagine you have a cold. You want to buy some medicine. One says it has a 90% success rate. Another says it doesn't help one out of every 10 people. Which would you choose?

Both have exactly the same success rate. The information is just presented in different ways. But most people would choose the first 5 medicine. This is called the "framing effect." The framing effect is not about "what you say"; it is about "＿＿＿＿＿＿ you say it." It can have a strong effect on consumer decisions.

The framing effect is commonly found in advertising. Marketers use it to make facts about their products **sound better**. They also use 10 the framing effect to make the prices of their products seem lower. A membership that costs $350 a year might **sound too expensive**. But how about "less than a dollar a day"? It **sounds much cheaper**!

So, next time you buy something, don't be fooled by the framing effect! 15

Reading Comprehension

1 **What is the passage mainly about?**

   a. the factors that affect customers' decisions

   b. the reason advertisements often use numbers

   c. advice on buying products at reasonable prices

   d. a way of making products seem more attractive

2 **What is the best choice for the blank?**

   a. why　　　　**b.** how　　　　**c.** when　　　　**d.** where

Writing Practice

3 According to the passage, how do marketers use the framing effect? Write two purposes.

   (1) to make _____

   (2) to make _____

4 **Which is NOT an example of the framing effect?**

   a. A restaurant charges $8 for a burger, but only $14 if a customer buys two.

   b. A doctor explains that 90% of his patients survive instead of saying 10% die.

   c. A health club advertises memberships as costing $2 a day instead of $60 a month.

   d. A shop says 2/3 of its customers are satisfied instead of saying 33% aren't satisfied.

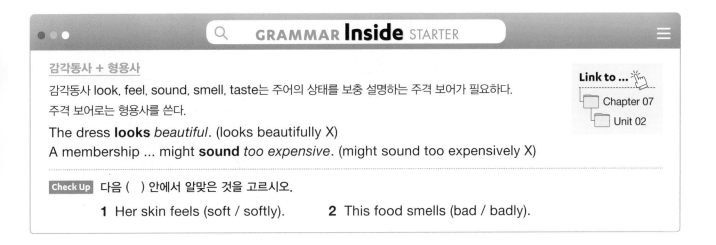

GRAMMAR **Inside** STARTER

감각동사 + 형용사

감각동사 look, feel, sound, smell, taste는 주어의 상태를 보충 설명하는 주격 보어가 필요하다. 주격 보어로는 형용사를 쓴다.

The dress **looks** *beautiful*. (looks beautifully X)

A membership ... might **sound** *too expensive*. (might sound too expensively X)

Link to ...
Chapter 07
Unit 02

Check Up 다음 ( ) 안에서 알맞은 것을 고르시오.

   1 Her skin feels (soft / softly).　　**2** This food smells (bad / badly).

A Servant's Dream

Martha Harper was a Canadian household servant with a big ambition. She worked for 25 years to save money for her own business. In 1888, she opened the first public hairdressing salon, Harper's Salon. 5

At that time, most women did their own hair at home. Doing hair in a salon was an innovative idea! (①) This **made** Martha's salon **a huge success**. (②) But Martha didn't want to hire employees to run her shops on her behalf. (③) So she came up with a different business model. 10 (④)

In 1891, Martha sold the right to use the name of her salon to other women. Instead of being paid by Martha, the women ran their own Harper's Salons! This method later became known as "franchising." In the 1920s, there were more than 500 of these salons worldwide! 15

Today, Martha's franchising business model is widely used. This pioneering businesswoman **made** the spread of huge global businesses such as McDonald's **possible**.

Reading Comprehension

1 **What is the best title for the passage?**

  a. The First Businesswoman in History

  b. The Unique Hairstyles of Harper's Salon

  c. Martha Harper: A Beauty Product Pioneer

  d. How the Franchising Business Model Started

2 **What is NOT true according to the passage?**

  a. Martha opened her salon in 1888.

  b. In the 1880s, women usually did their hair at home.

  c. Martha's customers told her to start more salons in other places.

  d. Martha paid her employees to open more salons in other cities.

3 **Where would the following sentence best fit?**

  | Her customers encouraged Martha to open more salons in other cities. |

  a. ①   **b.** ②   **c.** ③   **d.** ④

Writing Practice

4 **According to the passage, what did Martha do in 1891?**

  She _____ to other women.

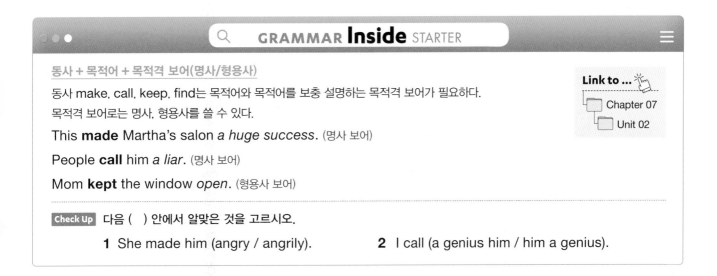

GRAMMAR Inside STARTER

동사 + 목적어 + 목적격 보어(명사/형용사)

동사 make, call, keep, find는 목적어와 목적어를 보충 설명하는 목적격 보어가 필요하다.
목적격 보어로는 명사, 형용사를 쓸 수 있다.

This **made** Martha's salon *a huge success*. (명사 보어)

People **call** him *a liar*. (명사 보어)

Mom **kept** the window *open*. (형용사 보어)

Link to ...
Chapter 07
Unit 02

Check Up 다음 ( ) 안에서 알맞은 것을 고르시오.

  1 She made him (angry / angrily).   **2** I call (a genius him / him a genius).

🔷 VOCABULARY INSIDE

READING 1	READING 2
☐ **success** ⓝ 성공 something that achieves a positive or desired result ⓐ successful　[antonym] failure	☐ **household** ⓐ 가정의 relating to a home or to the people living together in a house [synonym] domestic
☐ **consumer** ⓝ 소비자 someone who buys goods or services ⓥ consume　[antonym] producer	☐ **ambition** ⓝ 야망, 포부 a strong desire or wish to achieve something ⓐ ambitious
☐ **decision** ⓝ 결정, 판단 a choice that requires thinking or consideration ⓥ decide	☐ **hire** ⓥ 고용하다 to employ someone for a particular job [synonym] employ　[antonym] fire
☐ **low** ⓐ 낮은 below the normal or usual amount ⓐⓓ low　[antonym] high	☐ **run** ⓥ 운영하다 to manage or be in control of a business
☐ **cost** ⓥ (값·비용이) ~이다 to cause someone to pay an amount of money ⓝ cost	☐ **global** ⓐ 세계적인 relating to the entire world [synonym] international

Check Up　Fill in the blanks with the words above. Change the form if necessary.

1　She decided to _____ a restaurant.

2　The tickets will _____ $20 per person.

3　He's successful because he's full of _____.

4　You must not make a(n) _____ based on rumor.

5　We set a list of _____ rules before we got married.

6　On a(n) _____ scale, 77% of energy is created from fossil fuels.

7　We worked hard to prepare for the event, and it was a huge _____.

8　He will _____ some programmers to make an innovative application.

UNIT
03 | Jobs

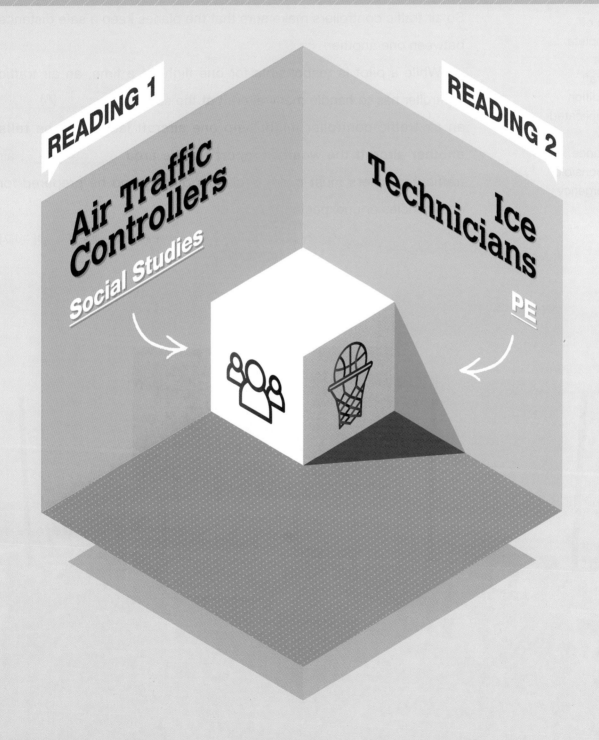

READING 1

Air Traffic Controllers

Social Studies

READING 2

Ice Technicians

PE

Air Traffic Controllers

A plane takes off from New York and lands in London. The pilot completed the flight safely — but he didn't do it alone. Many people are needed to make a safe journey.

One important job is *air traffic controller. Air traffic controllers keep radio and radar contact with the aircraft and **give the pilot information** 5 **such as weather conditions**. But there are more complicated duties as well. In busy periods, there can be thousands of flights every hour. So air traffic controllers make sure that the planes keep a safe distance between one another.

While a pilot is responsible for one flight at a time, an air traffic 10 controller has to handle many aircraft at the same time. _____(A)_____, an air traffic controller might help one aircraft land while he **tells another aircraft the weather report for the area**. _____(B)_____, air traffic controllers must make decisions quickly and be prepared for emergencies or unexpected events. 15

*air traffic controller 항공 운항 관제사

Reading Comprehension

1 **What is the passage mainly about?**
   a. how to become a pilot
   b. kinds of jobs at the airports
   c. the duties of an air traffic controller
   d. problems caused by heavy air traffic

2 **How does the writer introduce the topic?**
   a. by explaining a difficult concept
   b. by asking an interesting question
   c. by giving an example of a situation
   d. by giving a quotation from a famous person

Writing Practice

3 **According to the passage, how do air traffic controllers keep flights safe when there are a lot of flights at once?**
   They make sure that the planes _____ .

4 **What is the best pair for blanks (A) and (B)?**

(A)		(B)
a. For instance	—	Also
b. Otherwise	—	Therefore
c. In addition	—	As a result
d. However	—	In other words

● ● ●   🔍 **GRAMMAR Inside** STARTER   ≡

수여동사 + 간접목적어 + 직접목적어

give, tell, lend, show, send, teach, make, buy, ask 등은 간접목적어(~에게)와 직접목적어(…을)가 모두 필요한 수여동사로 쓰일 수 있다.

Air traffic controllers ... **give** *the pilot* *information such as weather conditions*.
                                 간접목적어   직접목적어

Brian **showed** *me* *his album*.
               간접목적어 직접목적어

Link to ...
⌐ Chapter 07
⌐ Unit 01

Check Up 우리말과 일치하도록 ( ) 안에 주어진 말을 바르게 배열하시오.

   나는 그에게 크리스마스 카드를 보냈다. (sent / I / a Christmas card / him)
   → _____ .

Ice Technicians

*How does good ice **allow** skaters **to perform** better? Today, ice technician Ralph Lewis is here to tell us.*

Q: What do you do as an ice technician?

A: I take care of ice rinks. First, I cool the concrete and carefully 5 spray water on it to layer the ice. Then I remove any dust with a machine. Finally, I check the rink's temperature, humidity, and lighting, as they affect the ice.

Q: What is important to do in your job?

A: It's important to _____ for each 10 sport. Speed skaters step hard and turn fast on the ice. Thinner and colder ice **allows** them **to do this**. However, figure skaters would hurt themselves from jumping on that ice. For them, the ice should be thicker and less cold.

Q: Is there anything you would like to say about your job? 15

A: Good ice **enables** athletes **to perform safely and skillfully**. I work hard for that.

Vocabulary

Check the boxes as you find the words in the passage.

- ☐ take care of
- ☐ cool
- ☐ layer
- ☐ remove
- ☐ temperature
- ☐ humidity
- ☐ lighting
- ☐ hurt
- ☐ athlete
- ☐ skillfully

Reading Comprehension

1   What is the passage mainly about?

a. what an ice technician does

b. how to become an ice technician

c. the ways athletes train at ice rinks

d. the reason athletes like different ice rinks

2   Arrange (A)~(C) correctly in Ralph Lewis's work order.

| (A) spraying water | (B) removing dust | (C) cooling the concrete |

_____ → _____ → _____

Writing Practice

3   According to the passage, what are three things that affect the ice?

The rink's _____, _____, and _____ affect the ice.

4   What is the best choice for the blank?

a. hire a new ice technician

b. adjust the ice's temperature and thickness

c. maintain the ice rink's humidity and lighting

d. improve the athlete's speed and jumping ability

○○○ ●   🔍 GRAMMAR **Inside** LEVEL 1   ≡

동사 + 목적어 + 목적격 보어(to부정사)

want, enable, expect, allow, tell, order, ask, advise 등의 동사는 목적격 보어로 to부정사를 취한다.

How does good ice **allow** *skaters to perform better*?
　　　　　　　　　　　目的語　　目적격 보어

Good ice **enables** *athletes to perform safely and skillfully*.
　　　　　　　　目적어　　　　목적격 보어

We **expected** *John to win the game*.
　　　　　　　목적어　　목적격 보어

Link to ... 👆
　Chapter 05
　Unit 03

Check Up 우리말과 일치하도록 ( ) 안에 주어진 말을 바르게 배열하시오.

Tom은 나에게 많은 책을 읽으라고 충고했다. (to / me / Tom / read / advised)

→ _____ a lot of books.

VOCABULARY INSIDE

READING 1	READING 2
☐ **take off** 이륙하다 to leave the ground and begin to fly [antonym] land	☐ **cool** ⓥ 차갑게 하다 to lower the temperature of something [antonym] warm
☐ **complete** ⓥ 완료하다, 끝마치다 to finish doing something or making something ⓐ complete　ⓝ completion	☐ **remove** ⓥ 제거하다 to take something out of or away from a place ⓝ removal　[synonym] eliminate
☐ **duty** ⓝ 임무, 직무 something that needs to be done as part of a job	☐ **temperature** ⓝ 온도 a measurement of how hot or cold something is
☐ **responsible** ⓐ 책임이 있는 having the job or duty of taking care of something ⓝ responsibility	☐ **hurt** ⓥ 다치게 하다 to cause pain or injury to yourself or someone else [synonym] injure
☐ **emergency** ⓝ 응급 (상황) an unexpected and dangerous situation that requires immediate action	☐ **athlete** ⓝ 운동선수 a person who is good at sports and competes in sporting events ⓐ athletic

Check Up　**Fill in the blanks with the words above. Change the form if necessary.**

1　The _____ will drop to −10°C today.

2　He is _____ for designing the website.

3　I drank a lot of cold water to _____ myself down.

4　_____ all the dust on the table and place the dough.

5　The boy ran too fast and fell down. He _____ his leg.

6　Firefighters raced to the site in response to the _____ call.

7　Did you _____ the homework for science class for tomorrow?

8　The _____ took part in a national competition. He won a silver medal.

UNIT
04 | Technology

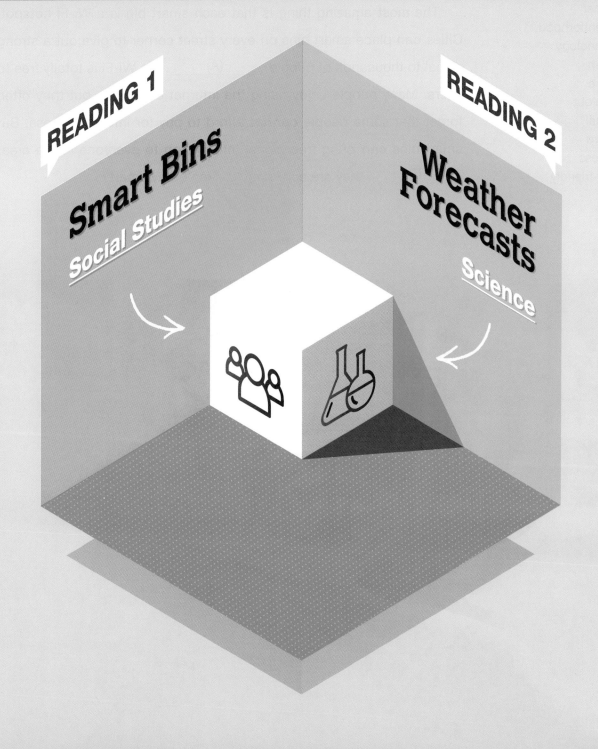

Smart Bins

Something new is coming to city streets. In Singapore and New York, you **can** already see one on many street corners. It is the "smart bin," a high-tech trash can.

A smart bin makes a neighborhood better in several ways. With solar-power technology, it crushes trash. This way, it **can** hold more 5 trash. And its special sensors tell the trash collection team when it is full.

The most amazing thing is that each smart bin is a Wi-Fi hotspot. Cities **can** place smart bins on every street corner to give out a strong signal to thousands of people. _____(A)_____, the Wi-Fi is totally free to 10 users. Many people enjoy using the internet every day, but they often forget that some people **cannot** afford to pay for internet access. But smart bins **can** bring free digital information to everyone in the area. _____(B)_____, they are eco-friendly. Aren't they smart?

Reading Comprehension

1 What is the passage mainly about?

   a. a new policy to keep streets clean

   b. ways to get free digital information

   c. the importance of equal internet access

   d. a new type of trash can that makes cities better

2 What is NOT true about smart bins?

   a. They use solar power.

   b. They hold more trash than regular bins.

   c. They can regularly empty themselves.

   d. They provide free Wi-Fi.

3 What is the best pair for blanks (A) and (B)?

(A)	(B)	(A)	(B)
a. Still — In addition		b. Still — However	
c. Best of all — However		d. Best of all — In addition	

Writing Practice

4 According to the passage, what can smart bins bring to everyone in the area?

   They can bring _____ to everyone.

GRAMMAR Inside STARTER

조동사 can

- 조동사는 동사 앞에 쓰여 동사에 〈능력〉, 〈허가〉, 〈의무〉 등의 의미를 더한다.
- 조동사 can은 〈가능〉, 〈능력〉, 〈허가〉를 의미하며 「can + 동사원형」의 형태로 쓰인다.

  ..., you **can** already *see* one on many street corners. (가능)

  ..., it **can** *hold* more trash. (능력)   You **can** *go* home now. (허가)

  Peter **can't[cannot]** *play* the piano. (부정형, 능력)

Link to ...
  Chapter 08
  Unit 01

Check Up 다음 ( ) 안에서 알맞은 것을 고르시오.

   1 He cannot (fix / fixes) that computer.

   2 I read the book. So I (can / can't) tell you about it.

Technology

142 words

Science

Weather Forecasts

ⓥ **Vocabulary**

Check the boxes as you
find the words in the
passage.

☐ forecast
☐ grab
☐ prediction
☐ condition
☐ expect
☐ accurate
☐ instrument
☐ process
☐ compare
☐ result

You put your shoes on and grab your school bag. Just as you open
the door to leave, your mom says, "You should take your umbrella. It's
going to rain today." Can she see into the future? No! she just checked
the weather forecast.

Weather forecasts give us predictions about the weather. They can 5
help us make decisions about the clothes we wear. And they can also
warn us if dangerous weather conditions are expected.

Weather forecasts are created by people called *meteorologists.
(①) To make accurate predictions, they **have to** use tons of
information from highly advanced weather stations. (②) These weather 10
stations collect information from many places. (③) For example, they
get data from special instruments on boats and airplanes. (④)

To process the data, meteorologists **must** use a supercomputer.
Then they can compare the results with previous weather patterns to
make their predictions. 15

*meteorologist 기상학자

Reading Comprehension

1 **What is the passage mainly about?**
 a. ways to prepare for bad weather
 b. advances in prediction technology
 c. why weather stations are important
 d. how meteorologists predict the weather

2 **Find the word from the passage that has the given meaning.**

a prediction about something, usually based on known information

_____

3 **Where would the following sentence best fit?**

Weather balloons and satellites send them data as well.

 a. ①   **b.** ②   **c.** ③   **d.** ④

Writing Practice

4 **According to the passage, what can meteorologists do using a supercomputer?**
 They can _____ to make their predictions.

● ●   🔍 **GRAMMAR Inside** STARTER   ≡

조동사 must, have/has to

• must와 have/has to는 〈의무〉를 나타내는 조동사로 '~해야 한다'의 의미이다.

 ..., meteorologists **must** _use_ a supercomputer.

 ..., they **have to** _use_ tons of information from highly advanced weather stations.

• must의 부정형인 must not은 '~해서는 안 된다'의 의미인 반면, have/has to의 부정형인 don't/doesn't have to는
'~할 필요가 없다'의 의미이다.

 You **must not** _pick_ the flowers.

 He **doesn't have to** _pay_. I've already paid for it.

Link to ... 👆
 📁 Chapter 08
 📁 Unit 02

Check Up 다음 ( ) 안에서 알맞은 것을 고르시오.

 You (must not / don't have to) come to my house now. You can come later instead.

⬡ VOCABULARY INSIDE

READING 1	READING 2
☐ **neighborhood** ⓝ 동네, 이웃 an area of a town or city	☐ **grab** ⓥ 붙잡다, 움켜잡다 to take hold of something with your hand synonym seize
☐ **crush** ⓥ 눌러 부수다, 찌부러뜨리다 to press something so hard that it breaks or loses its shape	☐ **expect** ⓥ 예상하다 to believe or think something will happen ⓝ expectation synonym predict
☐ **signal** ⓝ 신호 a message or sound that is carried by a wave of light, sound, or something else	☐ **accurate** ⓐ 정확한 without errors or mistakes synonym correct antonym false
☐ **afford** ⓥ ~할 형편이 되다 to have enough money to pay for something ⓐ affordable	☐ **compare** ⓥ 비교하다 to examine how people or things are similar and how they are different ⓝ comparison
☐ **access** ⓝ 접속 a method or way of getting to something ⓥ access ⓐ accessible	☐ **result** ⓝ 결과 something that is caused by something else antonym cause

Check Up

Fill in the blanks with the words above. Change the form if necessary.

1 I can't _____ to buy it. It is too expensive.

2 He can _____ an apple easily with his hand.

3 You should try not to _____ yourself with others.

4 Her gold medal is the _____ of years of hard training.

5 Liam tried to _____ the balloon before it floated away.

6 A huge shopping mall is under construction in our _____.

7 In this experiment, _____ measurements are really important.

8 All the rooms in this hotel have _____ to the internet for free.

UNIT 05 | Solutions

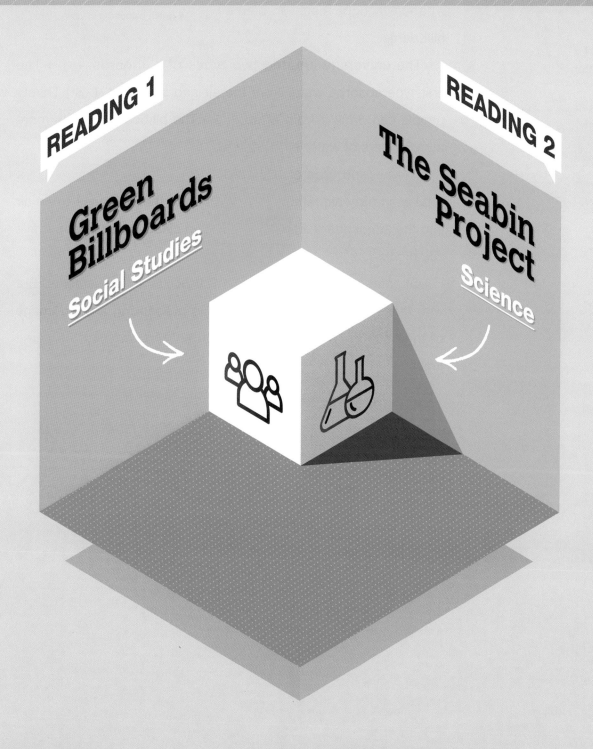

READING 1

Green Billboards

Social Studies

READING 2

The Seabin Project

Science

146 words

Green Billboards

V Vocabulary

Check the boxes as you find the words in the passage.

☐ billboard
☐ desert
☐ pollution
☐ local
☐ unusual
☐ absorb
☐ purify
☐ collect
☐ release
☐ atmosphere

Life isn't easy in Lima, the capital of Peru. The city is located in a desert, so it has little water. Also, air pollution **is increasing** due to heavy traffic. But a local university has created an unusual weapon to fight these problems: billboards.

▲ green billboards in Lima, Peru

5

The university created two types of billboards. (①) The first type absorbs water from the air and purifies it. (②) Thirsty people can drink it from a tap. (③) The billboard collects more than 90 liters of water every day. (④)

10

The second type of billboard _____. It takes in dirty air, removes pollution, and then releases clean air into the atmosphere. Each billboard can clean the air of about five city blocks.

15

Of course, the billboards are still used as advertisements. But with these billboards, the university **is presenting** a good image of their school, and **providing** clean air and water at the same time!

20

Reading Comprehension

1 **What is the best title for the passage?**

   a. Advertising Effects of Billboards

   b. The Dangers of Air Pollution in Peru

   c. A University That Invented a Water Purifier

   d. Innovative Billboards for Clean Water and Air

Writing Practice

2 **What does the underlined these problems refer to in the passage? Fill in the blanks.**

   (1) Lima is located in a(n) _____, so it has _____ _____.

   (2) _____ _____ is increasing due to _____ _____.

3 **Where would the following sentence best fit?**

Then it stores the water in a tank below the sign.

   a. ①   **b.** ②   **c.** ③   **d.** ④

4 **What is the best choice for the blank?**

   a. filters the air   **b.** cleans the water

   c. causes heavy traffic   **d.** promotes the university

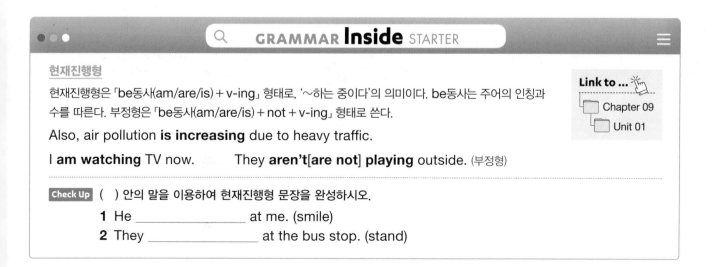

GRAMMAR **Inside** STARTER

현재진행형

현재진행형은 「be동사(am/are/is) + v-ing」 형태로, '~하는 중이다'의 의미이다. be동사는 주어의 인칭과 수를 따른다. 부정형은 「be동사(am/are/is) + not + v-ing」 형태로 쓴다.

Link to ...
Chapter 09
Unit 01

Also, air pollution **is increasing** due to heavy traffic.

I **am watching** TV now.   They **aren't[are not] playing** outside. (부정형)

Check Up ( ) 안의 말을 이용하여 현재진행형 문장을 완성하시오.

   1 He _____ at me. (smile)

   2 They _____ at the bus stop. (stand)

The Seabin Project

The Seabin is a floating garbage bin. It was invented by Australian surfers to remove trash from the ocean. Once it's set up, ① it can collect garbage by itself and run for 24 hours a day!

The Seabin is made with recycled plastic. And ② it has a mesh bag inside made of natural materials. Ocean water is sucked through the bag with a pump, and then ③ it is released back into the ocean. But the garbage in the water gets caught in the bag, so ④ it stays inside the Seabin. **Attaching** 10 a special filter to the Seabin will also allow it to remove oil from the water! Each day, this amazing system can remove about 3.9 kg of pollution from the ocean.

Because it needs a pump, **using** the Seabin in open water isn't possible. So, you'll only see them used near land. But they are very 15 effective at **cleaning** the water around docks and harbors.

5

Reading Comprehension

1　**What is the passage mainly about?**
　a. tips for preventing water pollution
　b. a device used to clean ocean water
　c. different inventions made in Australia
　d. ways to remove oil from oceans and lakes

2　**What is NOT true about the Seabin?**
　a. It was created by surfers from Australia.
　b. It operates 24 hours a day.
　c. It is made with recycled plastic.
　d. It can be used anywhere in the ocean.

3　**Among ①~④, which refers to the Seabin? Choose two.**
　a. ①　　　　　b. ②　　　　　c. ③　　　　　d. ④

Writing Practice
4　**According to the passage, what will allow the Seabin to remove oil from the water?**
　_____ will allow it to remove oil from the water.

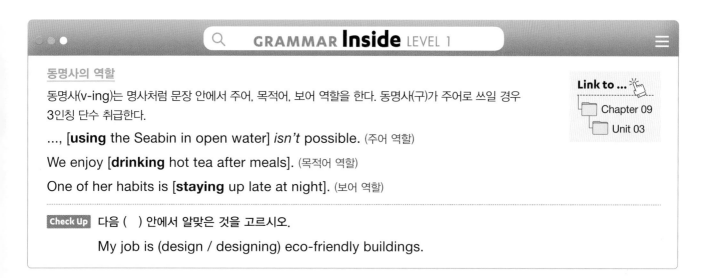

GRAMMAR **Inside** LEVEL 1

동명사의 역할
동명사(v-ing)는 명사처럼 문장 안에서 주어, 목적어, 보어 역할을 한다. 동명사(구)가 주어로 쓰일 경우 3인칭 단수 취급한다.

..., [**using** the Seabin in open water] *isn't* possible. (주어 역할)

We enjoy [**drinking** hot tea after meals]. (목적어 역할)

One of her habits is [**staying** up late at night]. (보어 역할)

Link to ...
Chapter 09
Unit 03

Check Up 다음 (　) 안에서 알맞은 것을 고르시오.
　My job is (design / designing) eco-friendly buildings.

VOCABULARY INSIDE

READING 1	READING 2
☐ **billboard** (n) (옥외의 커다란) 광고[게시]판 a large, flat sign for promoting something	☐ **run** (v) 작동하다 to work or operate synonym operate
☐ **desert** (n) 사막 a large area of dry land with little vegetation	☐ **recycle** (v) 재활용하다 to make something new from something that has been used before (a) recyclable
☐ **pollution** (n) 오염 물질 something that makes air, water, or the other part of nature unclean (v) pollute	☐ **attach** (v) 붙이다 to join one object to another (n) attachment
☐ **unusual** (a) 독특한, 흔치 않은 uncommon or rare synonym unique antonym common	☐ **possible** (a) 가능한 able to occur or exist (n) possibility antonym impossible
☐ **purify** (v) 정화하다 to make something clean from contamination (n) purification	☐ **effective** (a) 효과적인 producing a desired result (ad) effectively

Check Up **Fill in the blanks with the words above. Change the form if necessary.**

1 These pills are _____ in reducing fever.

2 I need some glue to _____ this note to the book.

3 We should _____ our trash to protect the environment.

4 The device will help reduce the level of _____ in the river.

5 She endured the extremely hot and dry weather of the _____.

6 The designer is famous for choosing _____ colors for his clothes.

7 Getting there by subway is not _____. You can only get there by car.

8 The building can _____ water and air on its own with its special system.

UNIT 06 | Cooperation

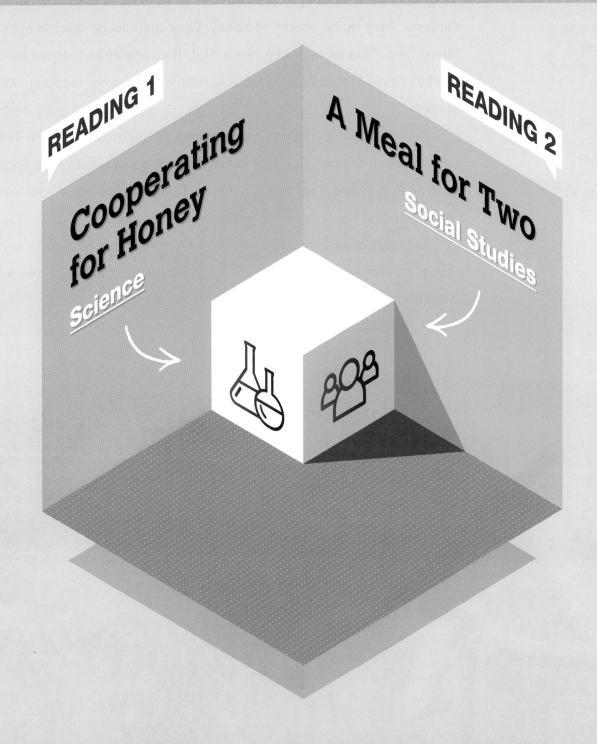

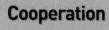

Cooperation

143 words

Science

Cooperating for Honey

Vocabulary

Check the boxes as you find the words in the passage.

□ cooperate
□ benefit
□ relationship
□ guide
□ calm
□ call out
□ nearby
□ leftover
□ diet
□ thanks to

Some animals benefit from having a special relationship with other animals. But have you ever heard of **one** between humans and birds?

Birds called honeyguides work with humans. Like their name suggests, **they** guide people to honey. Their main foods are the eggs, *larvae, and **beeswax in bee nests. But there are **ones** that are hard 5 to break open. In these cases, honeyguides have to work together with humans.

(A) At the nest, the humans use smoke to calm the bees. (B) The humans return the call and then follow **it**. (C) When a honeyguide finds a bee nest, **it** calls out to nearby humans. Then **they** break the nest and 10 take the honey. The honeyguide eats the leftover food.

The Hadza people of Tanzania are a great example of people who cooperate with honeyguides. About 10% of their diet is honey, thanks to the birds!

*larvae 유충   **beeswax 밀랍

Reading Comprehension

1 **What is the best title for the passage?**
 a. Where Most Honeyguides Live
 b. Why Some Animals Love Honey
 c. How the Hadza People Make a Living
 d. How Honeyguides Work with Humans

Writing Practice

2 **According to the passage, what is the main food source of the honeyguides?**
 Their main foods are _____.

3 **What is the best order of the sentences (A)~(C)?**
 a. (B) – (A) – (C)   b. (B) – (C) – (A)
 c. (C) – (A) – (B)   d. (C) – (B) – (A)

4 **Write T if the statement is true or F if it's false.**
 (1) Honeyguides easily break open all bee nests.   _____
 (2) Honey-hunting humans can calm bees down with smoke.   _____
 (3) When people find honey, they call out to honeyguides.   _____
 (4) Nearly 10% of the Hadza people's diet comes from honey.   _____

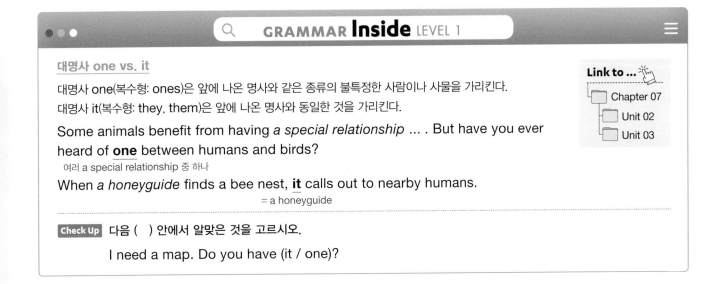

Q GRAMMAR Inside LEVEL 1

대명사 one vs. it
대명사 one(복수형: ones)은 앞에 나온 명사와 같은 종류의 불특정한 사람이나 사물을 가리킨다.
대명사 it(복수형: they, them)은 앞에 나온 명사와 동일한 것을 가리킨다.

Some animals benefit from having *a special relationship* ... . But have you ever heard of **one** between humans and birds?
여러 a special relationship 중 하나

When *a honeyguide* finds a bee nest, **it** calls out to nearby humans.
= a honeyguide

Link to ...
 Chapter 07
  Unit 02
  Unit 03

Check Up 다음 ( ) 안에서 알맞은 것을 고르시오.

 I need a map. Do you have (it / one)?

Cooperation

A Meal for Two

V Vocabulary

Check the boxes as you find the words in the passage.

- ☐ in need
- ☐ cost
- ☐ organization
- ☐ participate
- ☐ happen
- ☐ donate
- ☐ graduate
- ☐ proper
- ☐ convenient
- ☐ join

Helping someone in need doesn't always have to cost you extra time or money. It can be **as simple as** eating a meal at a restaurant!

A charity organization named Mealshare lets you do exactly this! To participate, visit a restaurant that is a partner with Mealshare. Then choose a Mealshare item from the menu and enjoy your meal. It's **as easy as** that! Every time this happens, the restaurant donates $1 to Mealshare. The money is used to give a meal to someone in need, at no extra cost to you! So you can "Buy One and Give One," as the Mealshare slogan says. 10

Mealshare was founded in Canada by business school graduates in 2013. They were unhappy that so many people couldn't get a proper meal, so they wanted to create a convenient way for restaurant-goers to help others.

In its first two years, more than 230 restaurants joined the 15 Mealshare program. And the number keeps growing!

Reading Comprehension

1   What is the best title for the passage?
  a. Serving Food to People in Need
  b. Mealshare: Eat a Meal, Give a Meal!
  c. The Best Restaurants for Busy People
  d. The Importance of Eating a Proper Meal

2   What problem does Mealshare care about?
  a. There are many people who cannot eat well.
  b. Many people don't pay after eating at restaurants.
  c. There is too much food waste in their community.
  d. People in the same community don't care about one another.

3   What CANNOT be answered about Mealshare according to the passage?
  a. When did it start?
  b. What is its slogan?
  c. How does it work?
  d. How much are its items?

Writing Practice

4   According to the passage, how many restaurants joined the Mealshare program in its first two years?

_____ joined the program.

Q   **GRAMMAR Inside** LEVEL 1   ☰

원급 비교

「as + 형용사/부사 + as」는 '~만큼 …한/하게'라는 의미의 원급 비교 표현으로, 두 대상의 양과 질, 또는 특성 등이 동일하거나 유사함을 나타낼 때 쓰인다.

Link to ...
  Chapter 08
  Unit 03

It can be **as simple as** eating a meal at a restaurant!

Next week will be **as hot as** this week.   James works **as hard as** Jenny.

Check Up 우리말과 일치하도록 ( ) 안에 주어진 말을 바르게 배열하시오.

이 스웨터는 저 스웨터만큼 크다. (as / this sweater / is / big)
  → _____ as that sweater.

VOCABULARY INSIDE

READING 1	READING 2
☐ **cooperate** Ⓥ 협력하다 to work with another or others ⓝ cooperation	☐ **organization** ⓝ 단체, 조직 a group of people with a particular purpose Ⓥ organize
☐ **relationship** ⓝ 관계 the way in which two or more people or groups are connected	☐ **happen** Ⓥ 일어나다, 발생하다 to occur, especially by chance synonym occur
☐ **guide** Ⓥ 안내하다 to show the way to someone or something ⓝ guide ⓝ guidance	☐ **donate** Ⓥ 기부[기증]하다 to give money or something else to help a person or organization ⓝ donation
☐ **leftover** ⓐ 남은 not eaten or used	☐ **proper** ⓐ 제대로 된, 적절한 suitable for the purpose or situation
☐ **diet** ⓝ 식이, 식단 the food normally eaten by a person or animal	☐ **convenient** ⓐ 편리한, 간편한 requiring little effort or worry ⓝ convenience

Check Up

Fill in the blanks with the words above. Change the form if necessary.

1 His poor _____ caused the disease.

2 We can make soup using _____ vegetables.

3 Delivery services make our lives more _____.

4 Two countries agreed to _____ with each other.

5 No one knows exactly what will _____ in the future.

6 The woman is the president of an international _____.

7 To maintain a healthy _____, people should be honest.

8 She decided to _____ her old toys and clothes to the charity.

UNIT
07 | Sports

On Ice?
No, Underwater!

ⓥ Vocabulary

Check the boxes as you find the words in the passage.

☐ underwater
☐ participant
☐ place
☐ signal
☐ hold one's breath
☐ opponent
☐ half
☐ substitute
☐ gain
☐ popularity

When most people think about hockey, they picture an ice rink. But next time you want to play hockey, go to a swimming pool instead. There, you can play hockey underwater!

Underwater hockey is a real sport with simple rules. Participants wear fins and snorkels. They also use hockey sticks to push the *puck, ⁵ but these sticks are **shorter than** ice hockey sticks. Before the game, the puck is placed in the middle of the pool. Players touch the wall above their team's goal and wait for the starting signal. When the signal rings, players hold their breath and swim. They score when they push the puck into their opponent's goal. Games have 15-minute halves, and ¹⁰ each team has six players and four substitutes.

Underwater hockey is gaining popularity with many people. This is because it is **safer than** ice hockey or field hockey. You might be surprised to hear that there are even players in their 70s!

*puck 퍽(아이스하키에서 공처럼 치는 고무 원반)

Reading Comprehension

1 **What is the best title for the passage?**

a. Health Benefits of Water Sports

b. Why It's Better to Play Hockey Underwater

c. The Importance of Following Rules in Sports

d. The Rules and Popularity of Underwater Hockey

2 **What is NOT mentioned about underwater hockey?**

a. the equipment used

b. the length of games

c. the number of players

d. the inventor of the sport

<u>Writing Practice</u>

3 **According to the passage, how do players score in underwater hockey?**

They score when _____.

4 **Why does the writer think that underwater hockey is gaining popularity?**

a. This is because it is safer than ice hockey.

b. This is because it is easier than ice hockey.

c. This is because it requires less equipment than ice hockey.

d. This is because it takes less time to play a game than ice hockey.

GRAMMAR Inside STARTER

형용사 비교급

• 비교급은 두 개의 대상을 비교할 때 쓰는 형용사, 부사의 형태이다.

• 형용사 비교급은 「형용사 + -er」 또는 「more + 형용사」로 나타내며, '더 ~한'의 의미이다.

Link to ...
Chapter 10
Unit 01

hard → hard**er**	short → short**er**	safe → saf**er**	b*ig* → big**ger**
hea*vy* → heav**ier**	good → **better**	bad → **worse**	many/much → **more**
little → **less**	famous → **more** famous	far → **farther**/**further**	

• 「형용사 비교급 + than」은 '~보다 더 …한'의 의미이다.

..., but these sticks are **shorter than** ice hockey sticks.

<u>Check Up</u> 우리말과 일치하도록 ( ) 안의 말을 이용하여 비교급 문장을 완성하시오.

이 신발은 저 신발보다 멋지다. (nice)

→ These shoes are _____ those shoes.

The Trampoline Effect

Sports

144 words

Science

❤ Vocabulary

Check the boxes as you
find the words in the
passage.

☐ wooden
☐ metal
☐ shape
☐ hit
☐ spring back
☐ cause
☐ bounce
☐ grass
☐ react
☐ professional

Crack! A baseball player hits a home run. If he uses a wooden bat, the ball will fly about 150 meters. But if his bat is metal, the ball will travel **more than** 200 meters!

In the past, all bats were made of wood. A wooden bat changes shape when it hits a ball and doesn't spring back. This causes the ball to lose some of its *kinetic energy. It's like bouncing a ball on soft grass. It doesn't bounce very high. 5

Today, however, many bats are made of aluminum. (①) Aluminum bats react differently than wooden bats. (②) An aluminum bat still changes shape when a ball hits it. (③) This makes the ball go **farther**. 10 It's more like bouncing a ball on hard concrete. (④)

Professional baseball players, however, must use wooden bats during games. They hit too many home runs when they use aluminum bats.

*kinetic energy 운동 에너지(움직이고 있는 물체가 가지는 에너지)

Reading Comprehension

1 **What is the passage mainly about?**
   a. how baseball players hit home runs
   b. the scientific facts behind the shape of baseballs
   c. the advantages and disadvantages of wooden bats
   d. why metal bats hit balls farther than wooden ones

2 **Write T if the statement is true or F if it's false.**
   (1) All bats were made of aluminum in the past.   _____
   (2) The shape of a bat changes when a ball hits it.   _____

3 **Where would the following sentence best fit?**

   | But it quickly springs back to its original shape like a trampoline. |

   a. ①   b. ②   c. ③   d. ④

Writing Practice

4 **According to the passage, why do professional players have to use wooden bats during games?**
   They _____ when they use aluminum bats.

Q   GRAMMAR Inside STARTER   ≡

부사 비교급
• 부사 비교급은 형용사 비교급과 마찬가지로 「부사＋-er」 또는 「more＋부사」로 나타낸다.

high → high**er**	fast → fast**er**	slow*ly* → **more** slowly
easi*ly* → **more** easily	well → **better**	badly → **worse**
much → **more**	little → **less**	far → **farther**/**further**

• 「부사 비교급＋than」은 '～보다 더 …하게'의 의미이다.
   ..., the ball will travel **more than** 200 meters!
   A snail moves **more slowly than** a sloth.

Link to ...
   Chapter 10
   Unit 01

Check Up 우리말과 일치하도록 ( ) 안의 말을 이용하여 비교급 문장을 완성하시오.

   Eric은 그의 여동생보다 더 열심히 공부한다. (hard)
   → Eric studies _____ his sister.

VOCABULARY INSIDE

READING 1	READING 2
☐ **underwater** ⓐ 물속의, 수중의 happening or found below the surface of water	☐ **wooden** ⓐ 나무로 된 completely or partly made of wood ⓝ wood
☐ **participant** ⓝ 참가자 someone who is involved in something ⓥ participate ⓝ participation	☐ **shape** ⓝ 모양, 형태 the outer form or outline of someone or something synonym form
☐ **opponent** ⓝ (대회·논쟁 등의) 상대 someone who is against someone else in a competition	☐ **cause** ⓥ 야기하다, 초래하다 to make something happen synonym result in
☐ **substitute** ⓝ 교체 선수 a player that replaces another player in a game	☐ **react** ⓥ 반응하다 to act in a particular way in response to something ⓝ reaction
☐ **gain** ⓥ (차츰) 쌓다[늘리다] to increase in some type of quality	☐ **professional** ⓐ 직업의, 전문적인 connected with a job that requires a high level of education or skill ⓝ professional, profession

Check Up — **Fill in the blanks with the words above. Change the form if necessary.**

1 She loved to carve _____ figures.

2 A submarine is a huge _____ ship.

3 The chocolate was in the _____ of a heart.

4 She worked hard and became a(n) _____ singer.

5 He kept crying. I didn't know how to _____ to it.

6 His extreme dieting can _____ serious harm to his health.

7 You will _____ weight if you eat a lot and don't work out.

8 All _____ said she was the most beautiful girl at the party that night.

UNIT
08 | Geography

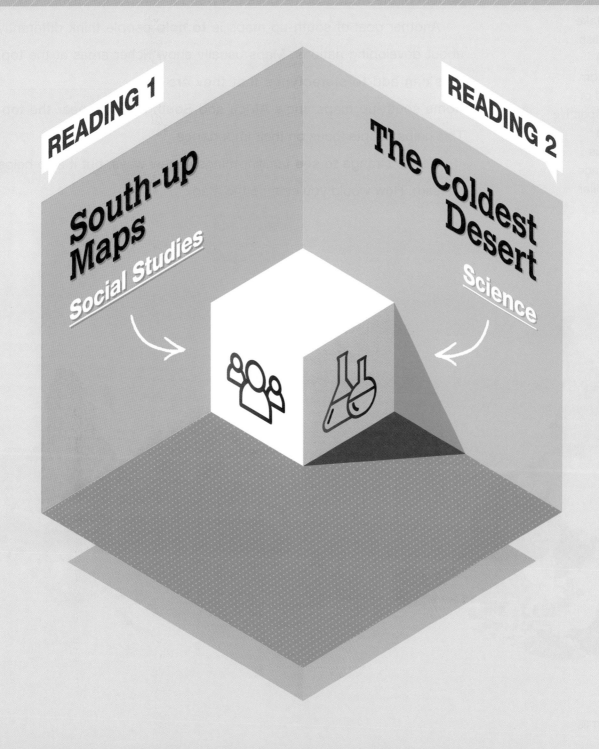

READING 1

South-up Maps
Social Studies

READING 2

The Coldest Desert
Science

South-up Maps

What do you think of the map below? Is it a mistake? No, it isn't. Actually, it's a south-up map.

In 1979, an Australian man, Stuart McArthur, published a south-up map. His goal was **to make** people think differently about his country. Many maps come from Europe, North America, or Asia. In these maps, 5
Australia is always at the bottom. McArthur was tired of being at "the bottom of the world." So he gave the world a new perspective.

Another goal of south-up maps is **to help** people think differently about developing nations. Maps usually show richer areas at the top. This can add to stereotypes that they are "＿＿＿＿＿＿＿＿＿." 10
Some south-up maps show Africa and South America near the top. This helps people focus on their importance.

It feels strange **to see** familiar things in new ways, but it also helps us learn. How would you change the map?

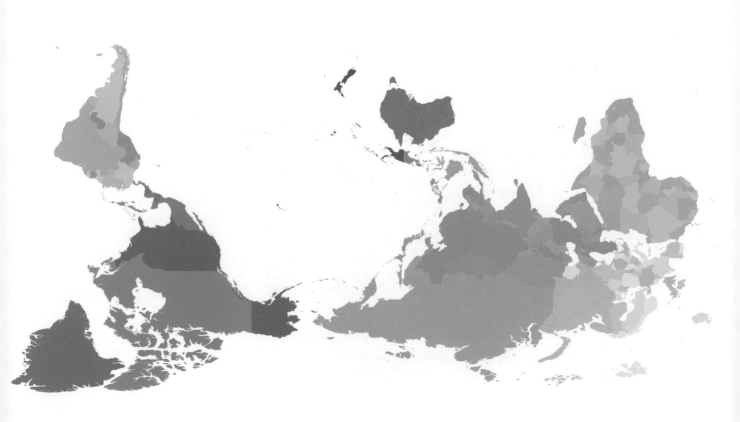

Reading Comprehension

1 **What is the best title for the passage?**
   a. A Perfect Map for a Tour around Australia
   b. Who Was the World's First Map Publisher?
   c. Buy a Map and Help Developing Countries
   d. See the World Differently with a Special Map!

2 **What does the underlined sentence mean?**
   a. McArthur wanted to be in a higher social class.
   b. McArthur didn't want to live in Australia anymore.
   c. McArthur was tired from traveling around the world.
   d. McArthur felt bad that his country was at the bottom of maps.

Writing Practice

3 **Find the word from the passage that has the given meaning.**

   > a fixed idea about what a particular type of person or thing is like

   _____

4 **What is the best choice for the blank?**
   a. bigger   **b.** more valuable
   c. cleaner   **d.** more traditional

Q   GRAMMAR **Inside** STARTER   ≡

명사적 용법의 to부정사

• to부정사(to-v)는 문장 안에서 명사처럼 주어, 목적어, 보어 역할을 하며, '~하는 것'이라는 의미이다.

   To see is to believe. (주어 역할, 잘 쓰이지 않음)

   She started [**to race** toward him]. (목적어 역할)

   His goal was [**to make** people think differently about his country]. (보어 역할)

• to부정사가 주어로 쓰이는 경우 보통 주어 자리에 가주어 it이 오며 「it ~ to-v」의 형태로 쓴다.

   To meet new people is exciting. → *It* is exciting **to meet** new people.

Link to ...
　Chapter 11
　Unit 01

Check Up 주어진 문장을 「it ~ to-v」의 형태로 바꾸어 쓰시오.
   To learn a foreign language isn't easy. → _____

The Coldest Desert

People usually think of deserts as hot, sandy places without many plants or animals. And since they don't have much water, people tend to believe they are very dry.

Many of the Earth's deserts fit this typical description. (A) For example, the Sahara Desert in Africa is one of the hottest places on 5 Earth. (B) In fact, the largest desert in the world is Antarctica. (C) But not all deserts are hot and full of sand. Instead of sand, Antarctica is full of ice. And it can get as cold as –89°C. Very **few** plants live there, so finding food is difficult. For this reason, most animals in Antarctica are meat-eaters. 10

The Sahara and Antarctica seem like really different places. But they both have very **little** rain or moisture. So living there is hard for plants and animals. As you can see, being hot doesn't define a desert. The main characteristics are _____.

Reading Comprehension

1 **What is the passage mainly about?**
a. the characteristics of deserts
b. how hot the Sahara Desert is
c. the hottest and coldest places on Earth
d. the differences between Antarctica and the Sahara

2 **What is the best order of sentences (A)~(C)?**
a. (A) – (C) – (B)　　　　b. (B) – (A) – (C)
c. (B) – (C) – (A)　　　　d. (C) – (B) – (A)

Writing Practice

3 **According to the passage, why are most animals in Antarctica meat-eaters?**
_____, so finding food is difficult.

4 **What is the best choice for the blank?**
a. being empty and having no plant life
b. being sandy and having very little rain
c. being cold and having very few animals
d. being dry and having extreme temperatures

Q　GRAMMAR Inside LEVEL 1　　≡

수와 양을 나타내는 형용사 few, little

• few는 셀 수 있는 명사와 함께 쓰이며, a few는 '조금 있는', few는 '거의 없는'의 의미이다.

I read **a few** *books* last month.　　　Very **few** *plants* live there.

• little은 셀 수 없는 명사와 함께 쓰이며, a little은 '조금 있는', little은 '거의 없는'의 의미이다.

I poured **a little** *milk*.　　　But they both have very **little** *rain* or *moisture*.

Link to ...

Chapter 08
Unit 01

Check Up 다음 ( ) 안에서 알맞은 것을 고르시오.

　1 I have (few / little) money. I can't buy that shirt.
　2 There were (a few / a little) people in the subway.

⬢ VOCABULARY INSIDE

READING 1	READING 2
☐ **publish** Ⓥ 발행[출판]하다 to produce and sell a printed work such as a book ⓝ publication	☐ **sandy** ⓐ 모래로 뒤덮인 made of, full of, or covered with sand ⓝ sand
☐ **bottom** ⓝ 맨 아래 (부분) the lowest part or level of something antonym top	☐ **typical** ⓐ 전형적인 being common or usual for a person, thing, or group ⓐ typically
☐ **perspective** ⓝ 관점, 시각 a way of thinking about or looking at something synonym viewpoint	☐ **description** ⓝ 설명, 기술, 서술 a statement giving information about someone or something Ⓥ describe
☐ **focus** Ⓥ 집중하다 to pay attention to something synonym concentrate	☐ **define** Ⓥ 정의하다 to identify the main qualities or meaning of something or someone ⓝ definition
☐ **strange** ⓐ 낯선 different from what is expected ⓐ strangely	☐ **characteristic** ⓝ 특징 a unique quality or feature of a person or thing synonym trait

Check Up **Fill in the blanks with the words above. Change the form if necessary.**

1 The newspaper didn't _____ my essay.

2 I wrote your name at the _____ of the page.

3 He gave a vivid _____ of the beautiful scene.

4 One distinct _____ of Seoul is its tall buildings.

5 They are playing volleyball on the _____ beach.

6 Wearing a coat in the summer seems quite _____.

7 Can you _____ the border between love and friendship?

8 Department stores should _____ on the needs of their customers.

UNIT
09 | Ice

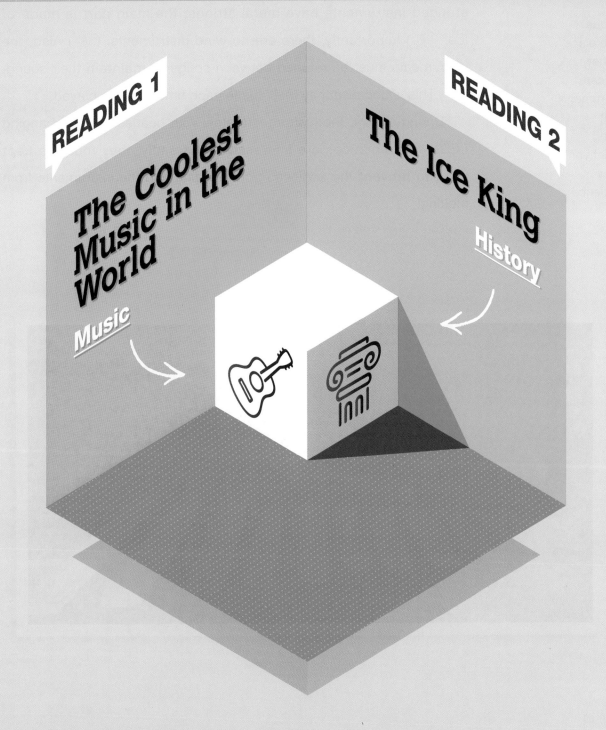

READING 1

The Coolest Music in the World

Music

READING 2

The Ice King

History

Ice

Music

The Coolest Music in the World

Every winter in northern Sweden, a unique performance takes place inside a frozen, igloo-shaped concert hall. People wear warm clothes and gather **to hear** the Ice Music orchestra. During the concert, each musician plays a delicate instrument. How delicate? One could melt in your hands! Surprisingly, the instruments are made of ice. 5

The Ice Music orchestra plays a variety of ice instruments, including violins, guitars, drums, and a large xylophone. (①) Although the stringed instruments have metal strings, the main part is made of ice. (②) Importantly, there are no wind instruments. (③) Also, the instruments must be retuned between songs **to maintain** their sound. 10 (④) This is because they melt a little each time they are played.

During shows, the instruments glow with heatless, color-changing LEDs. Performances are impressive. But sadly, they must be kept short **to prevent** the audience from freezing and the instruments from melting! 15

Vocabulary

Check the boxes as you find the words in the passage.

- □ unique
- □ take place
- □ gather
- □ delicate
- □ instrument
- □ melt
- □ string
- □ maintain
- □ glow
- □ audience

Reading Comprehension

1 What is the best title for the passage?

a. A Unique Ice Orchestra in Sweden

b. Sweden: The Best Place for Music Lovers

c. Build Your Own Musical Instruments with Ice!

d. An Orchestra that Appreciates the Beauty of Winter

2 What is NOT true according to the passage?

a. The orchestra is based in the northern part of Sweden.

b. Every instrument in the orchestra is 100% made of ice.

c. Wind instruments are not included in the orchestra.

d. The orchestra uses heatless lights during performances.

3 Where would the following sentence best fit?

> That's because they would melt from the musicians' breath!

a. ①　　　　**b.** ②　　　　**c.** ③　　　　**d.** ④

Writing Practice

4 According to the passage, why do the instruments need to be retuned between songs?

It's because they _____.

Q GRAMMAR Inside STARTER ☰

부사적 용법의 to부정사 (목적)

부사적 용법의 to부정사는 '~하기 위해'라는 의미로 〈목적〉을 나타낼 수 있다.

People ... gather [**to hear** the Ice Music orchestra].

Also, the instruments must be retuned between songs [**to maintain** their sound].

She ran fast [**to catch** the bus].

Link to ... 🖱

📁 Chapter 11

📁 Unit 02

Check Up 밑줄 친 to부정사구를 우리말로 해석하시오.

1 He went out to meet his friends.　→ _____

2 She raised her hand to ask a question.　→ _____

The Ice King

Vocabulary

Check the boxes as you find the words in the passage.

- ☐ refrigerator
- ☐ rare
- ☐ ship
- ☐ impossible
- ☐ store
- ☐ pack
- ☐ ancient
- ☐ free
- ☐ electric
- ☐ creativity

These days, ice is cheap and can be bought easily. But before refrigerators were invented, ice was rare. This changed when a Boston man, Frederic Tudor, began the ice trade in the 19th century. He came up with the idea **to take** ice from frozen winter ponds and ship it to hot parts of the world. People thought this was impossible. "It will melt!" they said.

▲ Frederic Tudor
(1783 ~ 1864)

5

At first, most of the ice Tudor tried to ship did melt. ① But later, he discovered a way **to store** the ice by packing it in *sawdust. ② This made it melt slower. ③ In ancient times, people stored ice in sawdust or salt. ④ Even when he shipped 180 tons of ice to Calcutta, India, most of it didn't melt.

10

To grow his business, Tudor _____. For example, he gave bartenders free ice **to try**. He knew people would love it! His business was a huge success until electric freezers were invented in the 1930s. Tudor's creativity and business skills made him rich!

15

*sawdust 톱밥

Reading Comprehension

1　**What is the best title for the passage?**

　a. The Invention of the Refrigerator

　b. The History of International Trade

　c. The Man Who Started the Ice Trade

　d. How to Make Ice Melt More Slowly

Writing Practice

2　**According to the passage, what does the underlined This refer to?**

Before refrigerators were invented, _____.

3　**Which sentence is NOT needed in the passage?**

　a. ①　　　　　　b. ②　　　　　　c. ③　　　　　　d. ④

4　**What is the best choice for the blank?**

　a. invented electric freezers

　b. marketed his product brilliantly

　c. lowered the price of his product

　d. opened a bar and used his product there

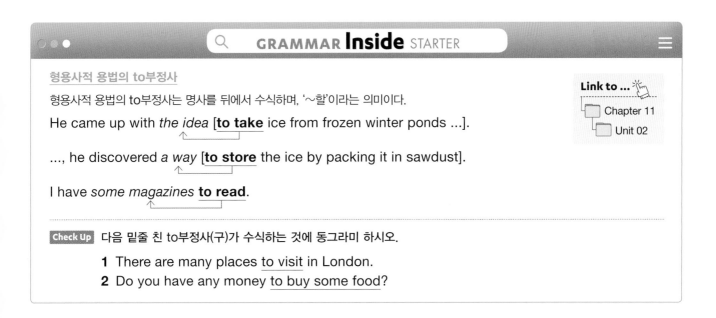

GRAMMAR **Inside** STARTER

형용사적 용법의 to부정사

형용사적 용법의 to부정사는 명사를 뒤에서 수식하며, '~할'이라는 의미이다.

He came up with *the idea* [**to take** ice from frozen winter ponds ...].

..., he discovered *a way* [**to store** the ice by packing it in sawdust].

I have *some magazines* **to read**.

Link to ...

　Chapter 11

　Unit 02

Check Up 다음 밑줄 친 to부정사(구)가 수식하는 것에 동그라미 하시오.

　1 There are many places to visit in London.

　2 Do you have any money to buy some food?

◈ VOCABULARY INSIDE

READING 1	READING 2
☐ **delicate** ⓐ 섬세한 주의를 요하는, 연약한 weak enough to be easily damaged [antonym] strong	☐ **refrigerator** ⓝ 냉장고 a machine that keeps objects, usually food, cold
☐ **instrument** ⓝ 악기 something used for making or playing music	☐ **rare** ⓐ 희귀한, 드문 very uncommon or unusual [antonym] common
☐ **melt** ⓥ 녹다 to become liquid through heat [antonym] freeze	☐ **ship** ⓥ 운송하다, 실어 나르다 to send something by ship ⓝ shipment
☐ **maintain** ⓥ 유지하다 to make sure something continues ⓝ maintenance	☐ **store** ⓥ 저장[보관]하다 to keep something somewhere safe [synonym] keep, save
☐ **audience** ⓝ 청중, 관중 a group of people who have gathered to see or hear something	☐ **free** ⓐ 무료의 costing no money [antonym] charged

Check Up | **Fill in the blanks with the words above. Change the form if necessary.**

1 The _____ sounds like a guitar.

2 Some animals _____ food for the winter.

3 She opened the _____ to take out some milk.

4 The _____ gave a huge applause to the pianist.

5 We _____ our products to other parts of the world.

6 Entrance is _____ for children under the age of six.

7 This plant is very _____, so you should take good care of it.

8 I try to _____ a balance between my work and personal life.

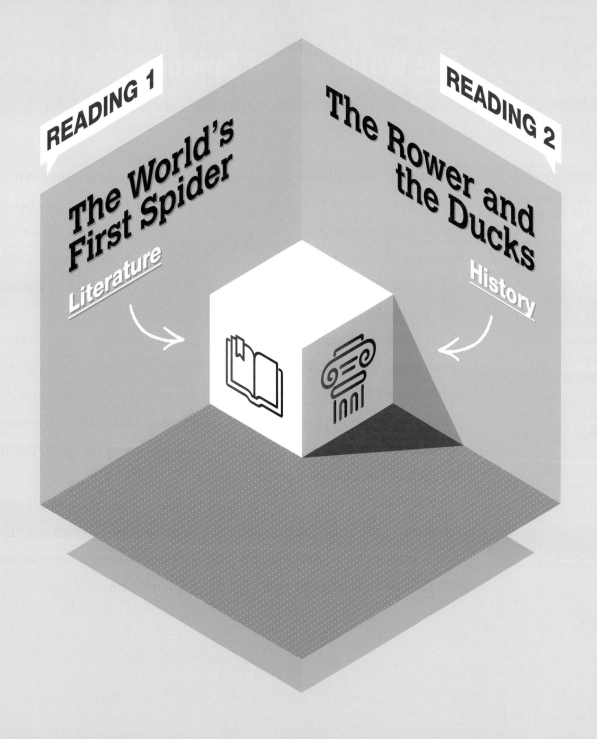

READING 1

The World's
First Spider

Literature

READING 2

The Rower and
the Ducks

History

The World's First Spider

ⓥ Vocabulary

Check the boxes as you find the words in the passage.

- ☐ talented
- ☐ weave
- ☐ brag
- ☐ boast
- ☐ disguise
- ☐ reveal
- ☐ challenge
- ☐ deed
- ☐ furious
- ☐ punish

Arachne was a young Greek woman. ① She was very talented at weaving and **loved to brag**. Athena, the goddess of weaving, heard about Arachne's boasts. ② She **decided to disguise** herself as an old woman and talk to Arachne. "Where did you **learn to weave**?" ③ she asked. "Was this talent given to you by Athena?" But Arachne replied, 5 "Of course not. I taught myself!"

This made Athena angry, so ④ she revealed herself as the goddess of weaving. "You **wish to challenge** me?" she yelled. "Then let's begin!" Arachne and Athena quickly **started to weave**. Athena made amazing images of the gods. In her pictures, they looked heroic and performed 10 good deeds. Arachne also weaved amazing images of the gods. But in her pictures, they were angry and foolish.

Arachne's pictures made Athena furious. "How dare you!" she screamed. "You must be punished." Athena grabbed a stick and hit Arachne. Magically, Arachne got smaller, grew legs, and became the 15 first spider! "Now you can weave all day," Athena said.

Reading Comprehension

1 **What is the best title for the passage?**
   a. The Disguises of the Gods
   b. Greek Gods: Heroic and Proud
   c. The Amazing Weaving Skills of Arachne
   d. Arachne and Athena: The Weaving Contest

2 **What is NOT true about Arachne?**
   a. She was very good at weaving.
   b. She said she taught herself weaving.
   c. She had a competition with Athena.
   d. She was a better weaver than Athena.

3 **Among ①~④, which refers to a different person?**
   a. ①　　　　**b.** ②　　　　**c.** ③　　　　**d.** ④

Writing Practice

4 **According to the passage, what happened to Arachne after Athena hit her with her stick?**
   Arachne got _____, grew _____, and became _____.

GRAMMAR Inside STARTER

to부정사를 목적어로 취하는 동사

동사 want, need, hope, wish, learn, plan, promise, decide, love, like, start, begin 등은 to부정사를 목적어로 취한다.

She was very talented at weaving and *loved* **to brag**.

She *decided* **to disguise** herself as an old woman ... .

Where did you *learn* **to weave**?

I *hope* **to see** you again.

Link to ...
Chapter 11
Unit 01

Check Up 다음 ( ) 안의 말을 이용하여 문장을 완성하시오.

1 He wants _____ a doctor. (be)
2 We decided _____ in Paris. (stay)

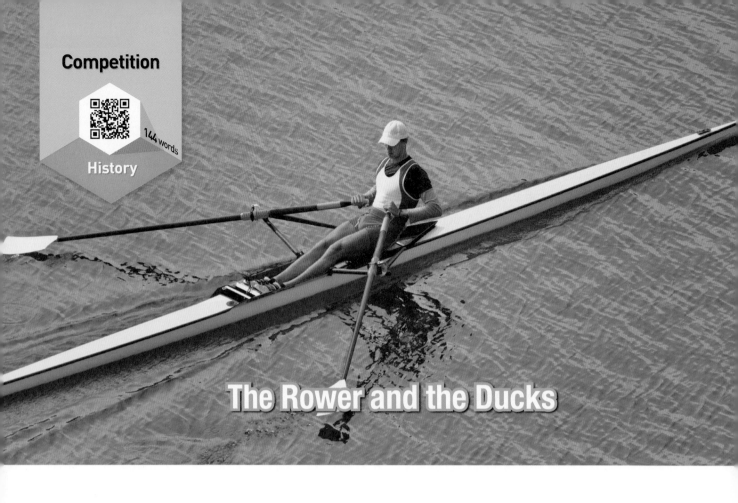

The Rower and the Ducks

Vocabulary

Check the boxes as you find the words in the passage.

☐ win
☐ compete
☐ event
☐ race
☐ cross
☐ opponent
☐ take the lead
☐ catch up with
☐ risk
☐ protect

Everyone likes to win. But some people understand that there are more important things in life than winning.

Bobby Pearce was one of these people. He was a great Australian rower. (①) In the 1928 Olympics, he was competing in the single *sculls event. (②) In this type of race, each boat has a single rower 5 with two **oars. (③) Halfway through the race, Pearce was winning easily. (④) A family of ducks was crossing directly in front of his boat!

Pearce didn't want to _____, so he **stopped rowing**. His opponent, however, **kept rowing** and took the lead. After the ducks had passed, Pearce **began rowing** again. Amazingly, he caught up with 10 his opponent and won the race!

Eventually, Pearce won the gold medal and set a world record for the event. But he **risked losing** the race to protect the lives of a family of ducks!

*sculls 조정 경기   **oar 노

Reading Comprehension

1 What is the best title for the passage?
a. Many People Want to Win!
b. An Athlete with a Big Heart
c. Ducks: The Solution to Winning a Race
d. The Meaning of a Gold Medal from the Olympics

2 What does the underlined sentence mean?
a. He used his skills to beat his opponents.
b. He was one of the best Olympic athletes in the world.
c. He was the type of person who would do anything to win.
d. He knew there are things that are more valuable than winning.

3 Where would the following sentence best fit?

> But then he saw something unexpected.

a. ①   b. ②   c. ③   d. ④

4 What is the best choice for the blank?
a. win the race   b. break the rules
c. hurt the ducks   d. give up the race

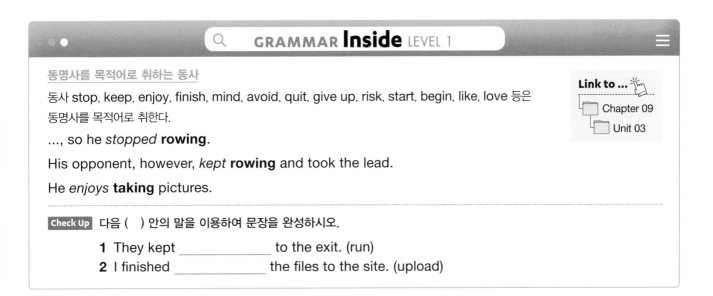

GRAMMAR **Inside** LEVEL 1

동명사를 목적어로 취하는 동사
동사 stop, keep, enjoy, finish, mind, avoid, quit, give up, risk, start, begin, like, love 등은 동명사를 목적어로 취한다.
..., so he *stopped* **rowing**.
His opponent, however, *kept* **rowing** and took the lead.
He *enjoys* **taking** pictures.

Link to ...
Chapter 09
Unit 03

Check Up 다음 ( ) 안의 말을 이용하여 문장을 완성하시오.
1 They kept _____ to the exit. (run)
2 I finished _____ the files to the site. (upload)

VOCABULARY INSIDE

READING 1	READING 2
☐ **talented** ⓐ 재능이 있는 having a special ability to do something well ⓝ talent	☐ **compete** ⓥ (시합 등에) 출전[참가]하다 to take part in a contest or game ⓝ competition
☐ **boast** ⓥ 허풍, 자랑 a statement in which you express too much pride in yourself or in something you have or have done	☐ **event** ⓝ 종목, 경기 one of the contests in a sports competition
☐ **reveal** ⓥ 드러내다, 밝히다 to show something that was hidden antonym hide, conceal	☐ **race** ⓝ 경주 a competition between people or teams to see which one is fastest
☐ **deed** ⓝ 행동 an action someone does	☐ **risk** ⓥ ~의 위험을 무릅쓰다 to do something that might be dangerous ⓝ risk
☐ **furious** ⓐ 격노한, 몹시 화가 난 extremely angry ⓝ fury	☐ **protect** ⓥ 보호하다, 지키다 to defend from attack, loss, or destruction ⓝ protection

Check Up **Fill in the blanks with the words above. Change the form if necessary.**

1 He didn't _____ the face behind the mask.

2 I was two hours late, so he was _____ with me.

3 Swimming is a popular _____ in The Olympics.

4 The best two teams will _____ in the next game.

5 I don't want to _____ going to dangerous places.

6 The police officers tried to _____ citizens from danger.

7 My mom always tells me to try to do a good _____ every day.

8 She is a very _____ musician. She got many awards in big contests.

UNIT
11 | Sea

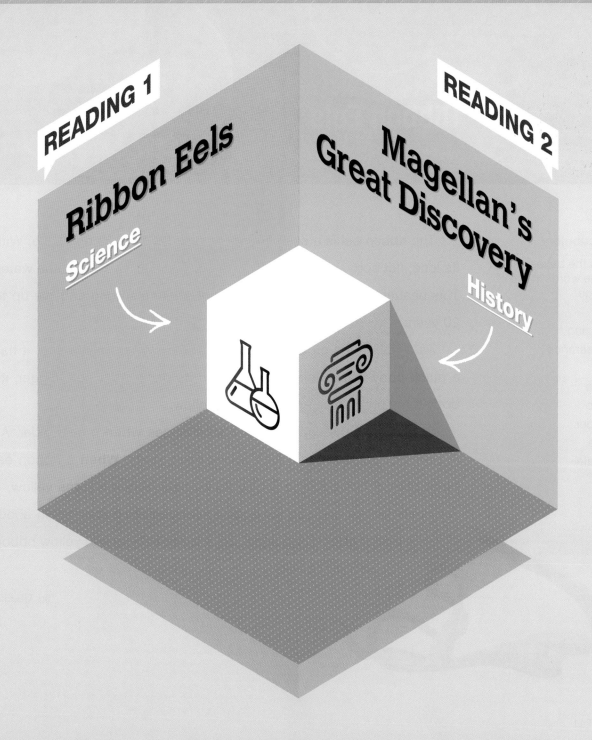

READING 1

Ribbon Eels

Science

READING 2

Magellan's
Great Discovery

History

Sea

151 words

Science

Ribbon Eels

V **Vocabulary**

Check the boxes as you find the words in the passage.

□ amazing
□ appearance
□ flat
□ wave
□ up to
□ gender
□ male
□ female
□ lay
□ wild

The ribbon eel is a sea creature with an amazing appearance. With its long, flat body, it looks just like a colorful ribbon waving in the water. This beautiful eel can grow to be about one meter long and live up to 20 years.

As a ribbon eel grows, its color changes. **When** it is young, it has 5 a black body with a thin yellow *fin on its back. As it gets bigger, its body turns bright blue and, finally, all yellow.

Surprisingly, the eel's gender also changes **when** it gets older. All ribbon eels are born as males with a black body. **When** a ribbon eel turns blue, it has become a fully adult male. **When** it turns yellow, it 10 becomes female and can lay eggs! Unfortunately, it dies within about a month **after** it lays eggs. So, it is not easy to find yellow ribbon eels in the wild.

*fin 지느러미

Reading Comprehension

1 What is the best title for the passage?
   a. Save Our Seas, Save Ribbon Eels!
   b. The Colorful Life of a Ribbon Eel
   c. Why Does the Ribbon Eel Have a Long Body?
   d. The Different Roles of Male and Female Ribbon Eels

2 Write T if the statement about a ribbon eel is true or F if it's false.
   (1) It has a long, flat body.   _____
   (2) It lives up to 20 months.   _____
   (3) Its gender changes when it gets older.   _____

Writing Practice

3 Fill in the blanks with the words from the passage to complete the chart.

The Changes of Ribbon Eels	
Body color	Gender
black	(1) _____
(2) _____	male
(3) _____	female

4 Why is it difficult to see yellow ribbon eels in the wild?
   a. because predators can find them easily
   b. because people keep them in aquariums
   c. because they die soon after they lay eggs
   d. because they are the same color as their surroundings

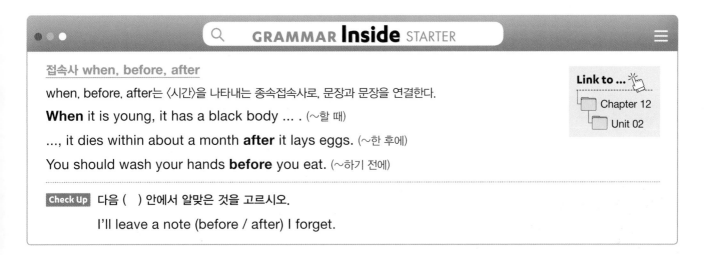

● ● ●   🔍 **GRAMMAR Inside** STARTER   ≡

접속사 when, before, after
when, before, after는 〈시간〉을 나타내는 종속접속사로, 문장과 문장을 연결한다.
When it is young, it has a black body ... . (~할 때)
..., it dies within about a month **after** it lays eggs. (~한 후에)
You should wash your hands **before** you eat. (~하기 전에)

Check Up 다음 ( ) 안에서 알맞은 것을 고르시오.
      I'll leave a note (before / after) I forget.

Link to ... 👆
📁 Chapter 12
📁 Unit 02

Magellan's Great Discovery

V Vocabulary

Check the boxes as you find the words in the passage.

☐ discovery
☐ major
☐ navigator
☐ route
☐ come upon
☐ calmness
☐ peaceful
☐ prove
☐ explore
☐ enormous

The Pacific Ocean is the deepest **and** largest of the five major oceans on Earth. The name itself was given by Portuguese navigator Ferdinand Magellan in the 16th century. He **and** his crew sailed from Spain in 1519 to find a route to the *Spice Islands of Indonesia. At the time, these islands produced the most pepper, **nutmeg, **and** ***cloves in the world.

▲ Ferdinand Magellan
(1480~1521)

5

During the voyage, his small group of ships came upon an unfamiliar ocean. _____(A)_____ its calmness, he called the ocean *Mar Pacífico*. This meant "peaceful sea," **and** the name "the Pacific" was derived from this. He believed the Spice Islands were very near, **but** that would prove untrue. Sadly, Magellan himself **and** most of his crew died at sea.

10

15

_____(B)_____ its name, the Pacific is a very active body of water. Countless unique creatures live beneath its great depths. To this day, we still haven't explored much of this enormous ocean.

*Spice Islands 향료 제도(인도네시아의 동부 술라웨시 섬과 뉴기니 섬 사이에 있는 섬들)
**nutmeg 육두구(육두구나무의 열매)   ***clove 정향(말린 정향나무의 꽃봉오리)

Reading Comprehension

1 **What is the passage mainly about?**
   a. the rich wildlife of the Pacific Ocean
   b. the way the Pacific Ocean got its name
   c. the reason Magellan became a navigator
   d. the difficulty of sea navigation in the 16th century

2 **What is NOT true about the Pacific Ocean?**
   a. It is the largest among the five major oceans.
   b. Ferdinand Magellan came upon it in the 16th century.
   c. The name *Mar Pacífico* means "peaceful sea."
   d. Humans have already explored the entire Pacific.

3 **Write T if the statement about Ferdinand Magellan is true or F if it's false.**
   (1) He started his voyage to find the Spice Islands in 1519.   _____
   (2) He discovered the Spice Islands and returned to his home country.   _____

4 **What is the best pair for blanks (A) and (B)?**

	(A)		(B)		(A)		(B)
a.	Due to	—	Despite	b.	Due to	—	Instead of
c.	Against	—	Because of	d.	Against	—	In addition to

Q **GRAMMAR Inside** STARTER   ≡

등위접속사 and, but, or

등위접속사 and, but, or는 단어와 단어, 구와 구, 그리고 문장과 문장을 대등하게 연결한다.

• and: 내용상 서로 비슷한 것을 연결하며, '~하고[그리고]'의 의미이다.

   The Pacific Ocean is *the deepest* and *largest* ... .

• but: 내용상 서로 반대인 것을 연결하며, '~지만[그러나]'의 의미이다.

   He believed the Spice Islands were very near, **but** *that would prove untrue.*

• or: 둘 이상의 선택해야 할 것을 연결하며, '~(거)나[또는]'의 의미이다.

   We can order pizza **or** *I can make one.*

Link to ...
📁 Chapter 12
  📁 Unit 01

Check Up 다음 ( ) 안에서 알맞은 것을 고르시오.

   I would take a vacation, (and / but / or) I don't have free time.

VOCABULARY INSIDE

READING 1	READING 2
☐ **amazing** ⓐ 놀라운 causing great surprise or astonishment ⓥ amaze ⓝ amazement synonym wonderful	☐ **discovery** ⓝ 발견 the act of finding or observing something before anyone else ⓥ discover
☐ **appearance** ⓝ 외형, 모습 the way that a person or thing looks on the outside synonym look	☐ **major** ⓐ 주요한 large in number, amount, or extent antonym minor
☐ **flat** ⓐ 납작한, 평평한 possessing an even or smooth surface	☐ **route** ⓝ 항로, 경로 a way to get from a starting point to a destination
☐ **gender** ⓝ 성별 the state of being male or female	☐ **peaceful** ⓐ 평화로운 calm, quiet, and free from disturbance ⓝ peace
☐ **wild** ⓝ 야생, 자연 an uncultivated area not inhabited by many humans ⓐ wild	☐ **explore** ⓥ 탐험하다 to travel through a place for discovery ⓝ exploration

Check Up

Fill in the blanks with the words above. Change the form if necessary.

1 The buildings are low and have _____ roofs.

2 This is a direct _____ to the downtown of the city.

3 He has the _____ power of recall anything he has read.

4 The neighbors' loud music ruined my _____ afternoon.

5 Plastic waste is a(n) _____ cause of environmental pollution.

6 The doctor made a great _____ in the treatment of lung cancer.

7 Jack worries obsessively about his _____, but I think he looks great.

8 The tigers were raised in the zoo, so they couldn't survive in the _____.

UNIT
12 | Environment

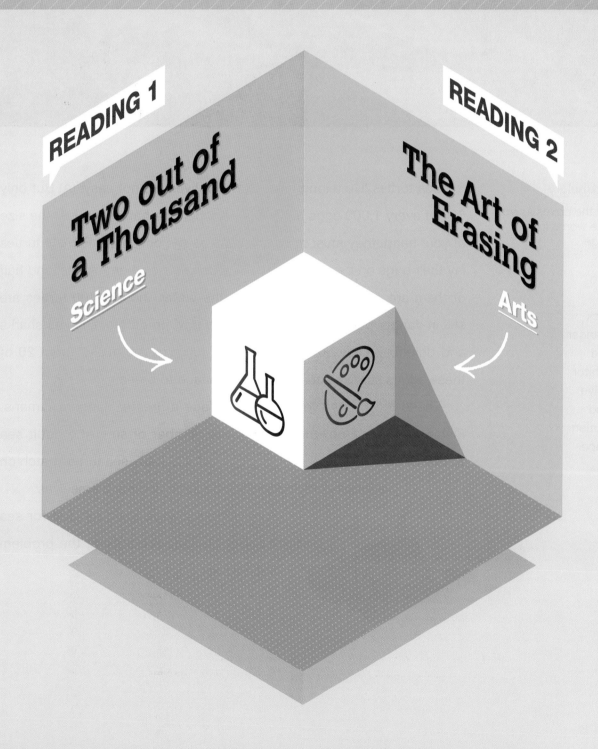

READING 1

Two out of a Thousand
Science

READING 2

The Art of Erasing
Arts

Two out of a Thousand

V Vocabulary

Check the boxes as you find the words in the passage.

- ☐ hatch
- ☐ lay
- ☐ attack
- ☐ in danger
- ☐ avoid
- ☐ predator
- ☐ survive
- ☐ breed
- ☐ pollution
- ☐ reduce

Sea turtles live a long time. But their lives are not easy. (A) But only 800 of every 1,000 eggs hatch. (B) Although the babies are just the size of your hand, they must make their way to the ocean. (C) Female turtles lay their eggs on beaches. They are attacked by other animals, and half of them are eaten. After they reach the water, the last 400 turtles are 5 still in danger **because** they must avoid new predators, such as sharks and dolphins. Only 50% grow to their full size. Normally, about 20 of these adults survive and return to the beach to breed.

These days, however, sea turtles face a greater danger: humans. Fishing nets and pollution reduce the number of surviving adult sea 10 turtles to just two. _____, **if** 800 baby sea turtles hatch on a beach, only 0.25% will become parents themselves.

Survival has always been difficult for sea turtles. But humans are making the problem much worse. 15

Reading Comprehension

1 What is the best title for the passage?
a. Life Under the Sea
b. Turtles' Struggle to Survive
c. How Pollution Affects Sea Life
d. The Mysterious, Long Life of Turtles

2 What is the best order of the sentences (A)~(C)?
a. (A) – (B) – (C)   b. (B) – (A) – (C)
c. (C) – (A) – (B)   d. (C) – (B) – (A)

3 What is the best choice for the blank?
a. However   b. Furthermore
c. In other words   d. On the other hand

Writing Practice

4 Fill in the blanks with the words from the passage.

> Of the 20 turtles that usually became parents in the past, only _____ now
> become parents due to the problems caused by _____.

GRAMMAR Inside LEVEL 1

접속사 because, if

• because는 〈이유〉나 〈원인〉을 나타내는 종속접속사로, '~하기 때문에'라는 의미이다.

..., the last 400 turtles are still in danger **because** they must avoid new predators, such as sharks and dolphins.

• if는 〈조건〉을 나타내는 종속접속사로, '(만약) ~하다면'의 의미이다.

..., **if** 800 baby sea turtles hatch on a beach, only 0.25% will become parents themselves.

Check Up 다음 ( ) 안에서 알맞은 것을 고르시오.

1 Feel free to ask me (if / because) you have any questions.
2 I'll help you this time (if / because) you helped me last time.

Link to ...
Chapter 11
Unit 03

The Art of Erasing

Most people think **that** graffiti is the result of adding paint to a wall or surface. But did you know **that** it's also possible to create graffiti by erasing something? This type of art is called reverse graffiti.

Reverse graffiti, also known as clean graffiti, literally reverses 5 the idea of traditional graffiti. First, reverse graffiti artists find a dirty surface. Then they clean away parts of the dirt with brushes and water hoses. Images are made by the contrast between the clean part and the dirty part. Reverse graffiti has been seen on dirty road signs and dirty tunnel walls, and this new trend is spreading all over the world. 10

Recently, reverse graffiti has been used as a form of advertising. Advertisements such as posters and leaflets use lots of materials and create waste. _____(A)_____, reverse graffiti only requires brushes, water, and creativity! Also, it's temporary and doesn't use harmful paints. _____(B)_____, it's very environmentally friendly! 15

Reading Comprehension

1 **What is the passage mainly about?**
   a. environmental problems caused by graffiti
   b. the relationship between art and advertising
   c. the difficulty of cleaning away dirt on the street
   d. a type of graffiti that clears off dirt to create images

Writing Practice

2 **Fill in the blanks with the words from the passage.**

> Reverse graffiti artists find a(n) _____ surface, and then clean away parts of the dirt with _____ or water hoses.

Writing Practice

3 **What does the underlined this new trend refer to?**

_____

4 **What is the best pair for blanks (A) and (B)?**

	(A)		(B)		(A)		(B)
a.	Meanwhile	—	However	b.	Meanwhile	—	Meanwhile
c.	However	—	For instance	d.	However	—	In other words

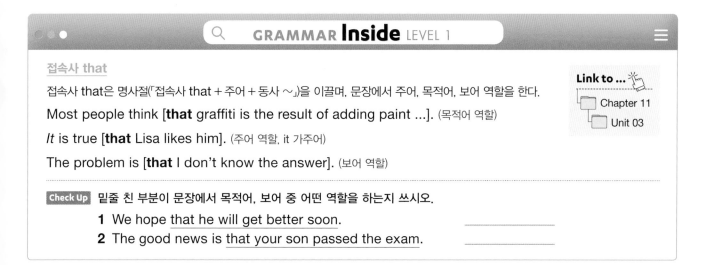

GRAMMAR **Inside** LEVEL 1

접속사 that

접속사 that은 명사절(「접속사 that + 주어 + 동사 ~」)을 이끌며, 문장에서 주어, 목적어, 보어 역할을 한다.

Most people think [**that** graffiti is the result of adding paint ...]. (목적어 역할)

It is true [**that** Lisa likes him]. (주어 역할, it 가주어)

The problem is [**that** I don't know the answer]. (보어 역할)

Link to ...
Chapter 11
Unit 03

Check Up 밑줄 친 부분이 문장에서 목적어, 보어 중 어떤 역할을 하는지 쓰시오.

   1 We hope that he will get better soon. _____

   2 The good news is that your son passed the exam. _____

VOCABULARY INSIDE

READING 1	READING 2
☐ **hatch** Ⓥ 부화하다 to come from an egg	☐ **erase** Ⓥ 지우다 to remove something [synonym] delete
☐ **lay** Ⓥ (알을) 낳다 to bring out (an egg) from inside the body	☐ **reverse** Ⓥ 뒤집다, 뒤바꾸다 to change something to an opposite position or condition ⓝ reverse ⓐ reverse
☐ **attack** Ⓥ 공격하다 to try to injure or kill somebody or something ⓝ attack [antonym] defend	☐ **form** ⓝ 유형, 종류 one of the types or kinds of a particular thing
☐ **survive** Ⓥ 살아남다, 생존하다 to stay alive or in existence ⓝ survival	☐ **temporary** ⓐ 일시적인, 임시의 lasting or used only for a short time ⒜ temporarily [antonym] permanent
☐ **reduce** Ⓥ 줄이다, 낮추다 to make an amount, size, or number smaller ⓝ reduction [antonym] decrease	☐ **harmful** ⓐ 해로운, 유해한 likely to cause damage ⓝ harm Ⓥ harm

Check Up

Fill in the blanks with the words above. Change the form if necessary.

1 The army _____ the enemy last night.

2 Fruit juices can be _____ to your teeth.

3 The female sits on the eggs until they _____.

4 Many artists insist that graffiti is a(n) _____ of art.

5 Look at that hen! She is _____ an egg into her nest!

6 Mom told me to _____ the time I spend on my phone.

7 You can't _____ aging and make yourself young again.

8 _____ shelters for the survivors from the earthquake will be built soon.

WORD LIST

UNIT 01 | Origins

O△X	a range of	다양한
O△X	advanced	형 진보된
O△X	afterwards	부 그 후에, 나중에
O△X	amazing	형 놀라운, 굉장한
O△X	begin	동 시작되다, 시작하다
O△X	birth	명 탄생, 출생
O△X	capture	동 붙잡다, 포획하다
O△X	chest	명 가슴, 흉부
O△X	coastal	형 연안[해안]의
O△X	consult	동 상담하다
O△X	discovery	명 발견
O△X	eventually	부 결국
O△X	for free	무료로
O△X	heart	명 심장
O△X	hollow	형 (속이) 빈
O△X	impressive	형 인상적인, 감명 깊은
O△X	inspire	동 영감을 주다
O△X	instrument	명 기구; 악기
O△X	loud	형 (소리가) 큰, 시끄러운
O△X	metal	명 금속
O△X	miss	동 그리워하다
O△X	modern	형 현대의, 근대의
O△X	noise	명 소리, 소음
O△X	patent	동 특허받다
O△X	plenty of	많은
O△X	produce	동 만들어 내다
O△X	rich	형 부유한; 풍부한
O△X	roll up	둘둘 말다
O△X	scrape	동 긁다
O△X	shipping	명 해상 운송
O△X	similar	형 비슷한, 유사한
O△X	spread	동 펼치다; 퍼지다, 확산되다
O△X	tiny	형 아주 작은
O△X	tone	명 어조, 말투; 음색, 음조
O△X	tradition	명 전통

UNIT 02 | Economics

O△X	advertising	명 광고
O△X	ambition	명 야망, 포부
O△X	business	명 사업
O△X	choose	동 고르다, 선택하다
O△X	come up with	~을 내놓다[제안하다]
O△X	commonly	부 흔히, 보통
O△X	consumer	명 소비자
O△X	cost	동 (값·비용이) ~이다
O△X	decision	명 결정, 판단
O△X	do hair	머리를 손질하다
O△X	effect	명 효과; 영향
O△X	employee	명 종업원, 직원
O△X	fact	명 사실
O△X	fool	동 속이다
O△X	franchising	명 가맹업
O△X	have a cold	감기에 걸리다
O△X	have an effect on	~에 영향을 미치다
O△X	hire	동 고용하다
O△X	household	형 가정의
O△X	huge	형 매우 큰, 거대한
O△X	imagine	동 상상하다
O△X	innovative	형 획기[혁신]적인
O△X	medicine	명 약, 약물
O△X	method	명 방법
O△X	on one's behalf	~을 대신하여
O△X	pay	동 (일의 대가 등을) 지불하다
O△X	pioneering	형 선구적인
O△X	present	동 제시[제출]하다
O△X	price	명 가격
O△X	product	명 상품, 제품
O△X	public	형 대중의
O△X	rate	명 비율, ~율
O△X	right	명 옳은 일; 권리, 권한
O△X	run	동 달리다; 운영하다
O△X	servant	명 하인, 고용인

WORD LIST

○△✕	affect	동 영향을 미치다
○△✕	as well	~도, 또한, 역시
○△✕	athlete	명 운동선수
○△✕	carefully	부 조심히
○△✕	complete	동 완료하다, 끝마치다
○△✕	complicated	형 복잡한
○△✕	conditions	명 (날씨 등의) 상태
○△✕	contact	명 연락
○△✕	cool	형 시원한; 동 차갑게 하다
○△✕	decision	명 결정, 판단
○△✕	distance	명 거리
○△✕	dust	명 먼지
○△✕	duty	명 의무; 임무, 직무
○△✕	emergency	명 응급 (상황)
○△✕	enable	동 할 수 있게 하다
○△✕	flight	명 비행, 여행; 항공기
○△✕	handle	동 다루다, 처리하다
○△✕	humidity	명 습도
○△✕	hurt	동 다치게 하다
○△✕	journey	명 여행, 이동
○△✕	land	동 착륙하다, 내려앉다
○△✕	layer	명 층, 겹; 동 층층이 쌓다
○△✕	lighting	명 조명
○△✕	one another	서로
○△✕	perform	동 수행하다; (경기 등을) 하다
○△✕	remove	동 제거하다
○△✕	responsible	형 책임이 있는
○△✕	safely	부 무사히, 안전하게
○△✕	skillfully	부 능숙하게, 솜씨 있게
○△✕	spray	동 뿌리다
○△✕	take care of	~을 관리하다[돌보다]
○△✕	take off	이륙하다
○△✕	technician	명 기술자
○△✕	temperature	명 온도
○△✕	unexpected	형 예상치 못한, 예상 밖의

○△✕	access	명 접근; 접속
○△✕	accurate	형 정확한
○△✕	afford to	~할 형편이 되다
○△✕	already	부 이미, 벌써
○△✕	area	명 구역, 장소
○△✕	bin	명 (쓰레기)통
○△✕	collect	동 수집하다
○△✕	collection	명 수집품; 수거, 수집
○△✕	compare	동 비교하다
○△✕	corner	명 모퉁이
○△✕	create	동 만들다, 창조하다
○△✕	crush	동 눌러 부수다, 찌부러뜨리다
○△✕	dangerous	형 위험한
○△✕	decision	명 결정, 판단
○△✕	equal	형 동일한
○△✕	expect	동 예상하다
○△✕	forecast	명 예보, 예측
○△✕	free	형 자유로운; 무료의
○△✕	give out	(소리·빛·냄새 등을) 내다[발하다]
○△✕	grab	동 붙잡다, 움켜잡다
○△✕	highly	부 고도로, 매우
○△✕	high-tech	형 최첨단의
○△✕	information	명 정보
○△✕	instrument	명 기구
○△✕	neighborhood	명 동네, 이웃
○△✕	place	동 두다, 놓다
○△✕	prediction	명 예측
○△✕	previous	형 이전의
○△✕	process	동 처리하다
○△✕	put on	~을 입다[신다]
○△✕	several	형 여러, 몇몇의
○△✕	signal	명 신호
○△✕	tons of	수많은
○△✕	totally	부 완전히, 전적으로
○△✕	warn	동 경고하다

UNIT 05 Solutions

O△X	absorb	통 흡수하다, 빨아들이다
O△X	advertisement	명 광고
O△X	atmosphere	명 대기
O△X	by oneself	자력으로, 도움을 받지 않고
O△X	capital	명 수도
O△X	desert	명 사막
O△X	due to	~ 때문에
O△X	effective	형 효과적인
O△X	float	통 (물에) 뜨다
O△X	garbage	명 쓰레기
O△X	heavy	형 무거운; 극심한
O△X	increase	통 증가하다, 늘다
O△X	inside	부 안에, 내부에; 전 ~ 안에
O△X	local	형 지역[현지]의
O△X	made of	~로 만들어진
O△X	natural	형 천연[자연]의
O△X	ocean	명 바다, 대양
O△X	once	접 일단 ~하면
O△X	pollution	명 오염 (물질)
O△X	possible	형 가능한
O△X	present	통 보여 주다, 나타내다
O△X	prevent	통 예방[방지]하다
O△X	provide	통 제공[공급]하다
O△X	purify	통 정화하다
O△X	recycle	통 재활용하다
O△X	release	통 내보내다, 방출하다
O△X	remove	통 제거하다
O△X	run	통 달리다; 작동하다
O△X	set up	설치하다
O△X	sign	명 표지판, 간판
O△X	store	통 저장[보관]하다
O△X	take in	~을 흡수하다
O△X	thirsty	형 목이 마른, 갈증이 난
O△X	traffic	명 교통(량), 차량들
O△X	unusual	형 독특한, 흔치 않은

UNIT 06 Cooperation

O△X	bee nest	벌집
O△X	benefit	명 혜택, 이득; 통 이익을 얻다
O△X	business school	경영 대학원
O△X	call out	~을 부르다
O△X	calm	통 진정시키다
O△X	case	명 경우
O△X	charity	명 자선 (단체)
O△X	choose	통 선택하다, 고르다
O△X	cooperate	통 협력하다
O△X	cost	통 (비용·대가가) 들다; 명 비용
O△X	diet	명 식이, 식단
O△X	donate	통 기부[기증]하다
O△X	example	명 예(시)
O△X	extra	형 추가의
O△X	follow	통 따라가다
O△X	found	통 설립하다, 세우다
O△X	graduate	명 졸업자
O△X	guide	통 안내하다
O△X	happen	통 일어나다, 발생하다
O△X	honey	명 꿀
O△X	human	명 인간
O△X	in need	어려움에 처한
O△X	leftover	형 남은
O△X	make a living	살아가다, 생계를 유지하다
O△X	meal	명 식사, 끼니
O△X	nearby	형 인근의, 가까운 곳의
O△X	organization	명 단체, 조직
O△X	participate	통 참여[참가]하다
O△X	proper	형 제대로 된, 적절한
O△X	relationship	명 관계
O△X	return	통 돌려주다; 대답하다
O△X	slogan	명 슬로건, 표어
O△X	smoke	명 연기
O△X	suggest	통 제안하다; 암시[시사]하다
O△X	thanks to	~ 덕분에

WORD LIST

□△✕	advantage	명 이점
□△✕	bounce	동 (공 등을) 튀게 하다; 튀다
□△✕	cause	동 야기하다, 초래하다
□△✕	disadvantage	명 약점
□△✕	effect	명 영향; 효과
□△✕	equipment	명 기구, 도구
□△✕	gain	동 (차츰) 쌓다[늘리다]
□△✕	half	명 (절)반; (경기의) 전반[후반]
□△✕	hard	형 단단한
□△✕	hit a home run	홈런을 치다
□△✕	hold one's breath	숨을 참다
□△✕	instead	부 대신에
□△✕	lose	동 잃다
□△✕	made of	~로 만들어진[구성된]
□△✕	middle	명 중앙, 한가운데
□△✕	opponent	명 (대회·논쟁 등의) 상대
□△✕	original	형 원래의, 본래의
□△✕	participant	명 참가자
□△✕	past	명 과거
□△✕	place	명 장소; 동 놓다, 두다
□△✕	popularity	명 인기
□△✕	professional	형 직업의, 전문적인
□△✕	react	동 반응하다
□△✕	require	동 요구하다
□△✕	ring	동 (소리가) 울리다
□△✕	score	동 득점하다
□△✕	shape	명 모양, 형태
□△✕	signal	명 신호
□△✕	soft	형 부드러운
□△✕	spring back	(원래의 모양으로) 되돌아가다
□△✕	substitute	명 대리자, 대용품; 교체 선수
□△✕	touch	동 (손 등으로) 대다, 만지다
□△✕	underwater	부 물속에서; 형 물속의, 수중의
□△✕	wooden	형 나무로 된
□△✕	the number of	~의 수

□△✕	actually	부 실제로, 정말로
□△✕	add to	~을 가중하다, ~에 더하다
□△✕	another	형 또 다른
□△✕	area	명 지역, 구역
□△✕	below	부 아래에, 밑에
□△✕	bottom	명 맨 아래 (부분)
□△✕	characteristic	명 특징
□△✕	class	명 반; 계층, 계급
□△✕	come from	~에서 나오다[생산되다]
□△✕	define	동 정의하다
□△✕	description	명 설명, 기술, 서술
□△✕	desert	명 사막
□△✕	extreme	형 극단적인
□△✕	familiar	형 익숙한, 친숙한
□△✕	fit	동 들어맞다
□△✕	fixed	형 고정된, 변치 않는
□△✕	focus	동 집중하다
□△✕	full of	~로 가득 찬
□△✕	goal	명 목표, 목적
□△✕	importance	명 중요성
□△✕	mistake	명 실수, 잘못
□△✕	moisture	명 습기, 수분
□△✕	perspective	명 관점, 시각
□△✕	publish	동 발행[출판]하다
□△✕	rich	형 부유한
□△✕	sandy	형 모래로 뒤덮인
□△✕	seem like	~처럼 보이다, ~인 것 같다
□△✕	stereotype	명 고정관념
□△✕	strange	형 낯선
□△✕	temperature	명 온도, 기온
□△✕	tend to	~하는 경향이 있다
□△✕	tired of	~에 싫증이 난
□△✕	traditional	형 전통적인
□△✕	typical	형 전형적인
□△✕	valuable	형 가치 있는

O △ X   O = I know this word and its meaning.
△ = I know either the word spelling or its meaning.
X = I've never seen this word before.
• Study the words that you've checked △ or X.

UNIT 09 Ice

O△X	ancient	형 고대의
O△X	appreciate	동 감상하다
O△X	audience	명 청중, 관중
O△X	a variety of	다양한, 여러 가지의
O△X	breath	명 입김, 숨
O△X	brilliantly	부 찬란하게; 훌륭하게
O△X	business	명 사업
O△X	come up with	~을 생각해내다
O△X	creativity	명 창의력, 창조성
O△X	delicate	형 섬세한 주의를 요구하는, 연약한
O△X	discover	동 발견하다; 알아내다
O△X	electric	형 전기의
O△X	frozen	형 꽁꽁 언
O△X	gather	동 모이다
O△X	glow	동 빛나다
O△X	heatless	형 열이 없는
O△X	huge	형 막대한, 엄청난
O△X	impossible	형 불가능한
O△X	impressive	형 인상적인, 인상 깊은
O△X	including	전 ~을 포함하여
O△X	lower	동 낮추다
O△X	maintain	동 유지하다
O△X	melt	동 녹다
O△X	pack	동 싸다, 포장하다
O△X	performance	명 공연, 연주회
O△X	prevent	동 막다, 방지하다
O△X	rare	형 희귀한, 드문
O△X	refrigerator	명 냉장고
O△X	ship	명 배; 동 운송하다
O△X	store	동 저장[보관]하다
O△X	string	명 줄; (악기의) 현
O△X	success	명 성공
O△X	take place	개최되다, 일어나다
O△X	trade	명 무역, 교역
O△X	unique	형 독특한

UNIT 10 Competition

O△X	beat	동 패배시키다, 이기다
O△X	boast	명 허풍, 자랑
O△X	brag	동 자랑하다, 떠벌리다
O△X	catch up with	~을 따라잡다
O△X	challenge	동 도전하다
O△X	compete	동 (시합 등에) 출전[참가]하다
O△X	cross	동 가로지르다, 건너다
O△X	deed	명 행동
O△X	disguise	동 변장하다
O△X	foolish	형 어리석은
O△X	furious	형 격노한, 몹시 화가 난
O△X	grab	동 (붙)잡다, 움켜잡다
O△X	halfway	부 중반부에
O△X	heroic	형 영웅적인, 용감무쌍한
O△X	in front of	~ 앞에
O△X	lose	동 잃어버리다; 패배하다
O△X	meaning	명 의미
O△X	opponent	명 (대회 등의) 상대
O△X	pass	동 지나가다
O△X	perform	동 (수)행하다
O△X	protect	동 보호하다, 지키다
O△X	punish	동 (처)벌하다
O△X	reply	동 대답하다
O△X	reveal	동 드러내다, 밝히다
O△X	risk	동 ~의 위험을 무릅쓰다
O△X	rower	명 노 젓는 사람
O△X	scream	동 소리치다
O△X	solution	명 해결(책)
O△X	set a record	기록을 세우다
O△X	spider	명 거미
O△X	take the lead	선두에 서다
O△X	talented	형 재능이 있는
O△X	unexpected	형 예기치 않은, 예상 밖의
O△X	weave	동 (베 등을) 짜다, 엮다
O△X	yell	동 소리치다

WORD LIST

UNIT 11 | Sea

O △ X	active	형 활발한, 왕성한
O △ X	appearance	명 외형, 모습
O △ X	be born	태어나다
O △ X	beneath	전 ~ 밑[아래]에
O △ X	bright	형 (색 등이) 밝은
O △ X	calmness	명 고요(함), 평온(함)
O △ X	countless	형 셀 수 없이 많은
O △ X	come upon	~을 우연히 발견하다[만나다]
O △ X	creature	명 생물, 생명체
O △ X	crew	명 선원
O △ X	depth	명 깊이
O △ X	derived from	~에서 유래된[파생된]
O △ X	despite	전 ~에도 불구하고
O △ X	discovery	명 발견
O △ X	enormous	형 거대한
O △ X	explore	동 탐험하다
O △ X	female	명 암컷
O △ X	flat	형 납작한, 평평한
O △ X	fully	부 완전히, 충분히
O △ X	gender	명 성별
O △ X	lay	동 놓다, 두다; (알을) 낳다
O △ X	major	형 주요한
O △ X	male	명 수컷
O △ X	navigator	명 항해사, 조종사
O △ X	ocean	명 대양, 바다
O △ X	peaceful	형 평화로운
O △ X	predator	명 포식자
O △ X	prove	동 판명되다, 드러나다
O △ X	route	명 항로, 경로
O △ X	surroundings	명 주변 환경
O △ X	unfamiliar	형 낯선, 익숙하지 않은
O △ X	unique	형 독특한
O △ X	untrue	형 사실이 아닌, 허위의
O △ X	voyage	명 항해, 여행
O △ X	wave	동 흔들리다

UNIT 12 | Environment

O △ X	add	동 더하다, 덧붙이다
O △ X	advertising	명 광고 (사업)
O △ X	attack	동 공격하다
O △ X	avoid	동 피하다
O △ X	beach	명 해변, 바닷가
O △ X	breed	동 (알·새끼를) 낳다
O △ X	clean away	깨끗이 치우다
O △ X	contrast	명 대조, 차이
O △ X	create	동 만들다, 창조하다
O △ X	environmentally friendly	환경친화적인
O △ X	erase	동 지우다
O △ X	face	동 직면하다
O △ X	female	형 암컷의
O △ X	full	형 가득한; 최대[최고]의
O △ X	half	명 (절)반
O △ X	harmful	형 해로운, 유해한
O △ X	hatch	동 부화하다
O △ X	in danger	위험에 처한
O △ X	last	형 마지막의; 마지막 남은
O △ X	literally	부 문자 그대로
O △ X	make one's way to	~로 나아가다
O △ X	mysterious	형 불가사의한
O △ X	out of	~의 밖으로; ~ 중에
O △ X	pollution	명 오염, 공해
O △ X	possible	형 가능한
O △ X	predator	명 포식 동물, 포식자
O △ X	reach	동 도달하다
O △ X	reduce	동 줄이다, 낮추다
O △ X	result	명 결과, 결실
O △ X	return	동 돌아가다
O △ X	reverse	형 반대의, 거꾸로 된
O △ X	spread	동 펼치다; 확산되다, 퍼지다
O △ X	surface	명 표면, 지면
O △ X	survival	명 생존
O △ X	temporary	형 일시적인, 임시의

Photo Credits

PAGE	PHOTO	SOURCE
p. 58	Frederic Tudor	https://en.wikipedia.org/wiki/Frederic_Tudor#/media/File:Frederic_Tudor-facingright_pre1864.jpg
p. 70	Portrait of Ferdinand Magellan	https://en.wikipedia.org/wiki/Ferdinand_Magellan#/media/File:Ferdinand_Magellan.jpg
p. 27	Part of a reverse graffiti by Paul Curtis(2008) in San Francisco, California, USA	https://www.flickr.com/photos/73852802@N00/2760825855
others		www.shutterstock.com

지은이

NE능률 영어교육연구소

NE능률 영어교육연구소는 혁신적이며 효율적인 영어 교재를 개발하고
영어 학습의 질을 한 단계 높이고자 노력하는 NE능률의 연구조직입니다.

READING Inside 〈STARTER〉

펴 낸 이	주민홍
펴 낸 곳	서울특별시 마포구 월드컵북로 396(상암동) 누리꿈스퀘어 비즈니스타워 10층
	㈜ NE능률 (우편번호 03925)
펴 낸 날	2022년 9월 15일 개정판 제1쇄 발행
	2024년 2월 15일 제4쇄
전 화	02 2014 7114
팩 스	02 3142 0356
홈 페 이 지	www.neungyule.com
등 록 번 호	제1-68호
I S B N	979-11-253-4030-0 53740
정 가	14,500원

NE 능률

고객센터

교재 내용 문의 : contact.nebooks.co.kr (별도의 가입 절차 없이 작성 가능)

제품 구매, 교환, 불량, 반품 문의 : 02-2014-7114

☎ 전화문의는 본사 업무시간 중에만 가능합니다.

READING Inside

Answer Key

STARTER

A 4-level curriculum
integration reading course

NE Neungyule

Answer Key

READING Inside

STARTER

UNIT 01 | **Origins**

READING 1　Listen to Your Heart

▶ **Reading Comprehension**
1 a　2 d　3 (1) T (2) F　4 all doctors should be able to use it for free

▶ **Grammar Inside Starter**
Check Up 1 went　2 came

해석　　1816년 어느 날, René Laennec이라는 이름의 프랑스 의사는 산책하러 갔다. 그는 두 소년이 속이 빈 막대기를 가지고 놀고 있는 것을 보았다. 한 소년이 핀으로 막대기를 긁고 있는 동안 그의 친구는 반대쪽 끝에서 듣고 있었다. 관 형태의 그 막대기가 아주 작은 소리를 매우 크게 만들고 있었다!

　　몇 달 뒤, Laennec는 심장병이 있는 한 젊은 여성과 상담하였다. 갑자기, 그는 그 소년들의 놀이가 기억났다. 그는 관을 만들기 위해 종이 한 장을 말았다. 그가 그것을 그녀의 가슴에 댔을 때, 그녀의 심장 박동을 또렷하게 들을 수 있었다! 그는 이 아이디어에서 영감을 받아, 나무로 된 기다란 관을 만들었다. 이것이 최초의 청진기였다.

　　그 후에, 다른 청진기들이 고안되었다. 1852년에, 뉴욕 출신의 의사 George Cammann은 두 개의 귀꽂이가 달린 금속 청진기를 만들었다. 그것은 현대의 것과 비슷해 보였고, 그 디자인은 그 후로 줄곧 사용되어 왔다. 그는 그의 청진기를 특허받지 않았는데, 모든 의사가 그것을 무료로 사용할 수 있어야 한다고 생각했기 때문이다.

어휘　heart ⑲ 심장　go for a walk 산책하러 가다　hollow ⑲ (속이) 빈　stick ⑲ 막대기　scrape ⑧ 긁다　tube-shaped ⑲ 관 형태[모양]의　tiny ⑲ 아주 작은　noise ⑲ 소리, 소음　loud ⑲ (소리가) 큰, 시끄러운　consult ⑧ 상담하다　roll up 둘둘 말다　chest ⑲ 가슴, 흉부　inspire ⑧ 영감을 주다　wooden ⑲ 나무로 된, 목재의　stethoscope ⑲ 청진기　afterwards ⑨ 그 후에, 나중에　design ⑧ 고안[디자인]하다; ⑲ 디자인, 설계　metal ⑲ 금속　earpiece ⑲ 수화기; *귀꽂이　similar ⑲ 비슷한, 유사한　modern ⑲ 현대의, 근대의　patent ⑧ 특허받다　for free 무료로　[문제] invent ⑧ 발명하다　discovery ⑲ 발견　advanced ⑲ 진보된　relaxed ⑲ 편안한　cure ⑧ 낫게 하다　heartbeat ⑲ 심장 박동　clearly ⑨ 또렷하게, 분명히

구문　**1행** ..., a French doctor [named René Laennec] went for a walk.
　→ [ ]은 명사구 a French doctor를 수식하는 과거분사구이다.

2행 He **saw two boys playing** with a hollow stick.
　→ 「see(지각동사) + 목적어 + 목적격 보어(playing 이하)」 구문으로, '~가 …하고 있는 것을 보다'라는 의미이다. 진행 중인 동작을 강조하기 위해 지각동사 see의 목적격 보어로 현재분사(playing 이하)가 쓰였다.

4행 The tube-shaped stick **was** *making* the tiny noise very loud!
　→ 「was/were + v-ing」는 '~하는 중이었다'라는 뜻의 과거진행형이다.
　→ 「make + 목적어 + 목적격 보어(형용사)」는 '~을 …하게 만들다'라는 의미이다.

8행 He rolled up a piece of paper **to make a tube**.
　→ to make a tube는 '관을 만들기 위해'라는 뜻으로, 〈목적〉을 나타내는 부사적 용법의 to부정사구이다.

9행 He **was inspired by** this idea, so he made a long, wooden tube.
　→ was inspired by는 「be + v-ed + by」 형태의 수동태로, '~에 의해 영감을 받다'의 의미이다.

14행 ..., and the design **has been used** ever since.
　→ has been used는 〈계속〉의 의미를 가진 현재완료 수동태로, '사용되어 왔다'의 의미이다.

15행 ..., because he thought all doctors **should be able to use** it for free.
→ '~해야 한다'는 의미의 〈의무〉를 나타내는 조동사 should와 '~할 수 있다'는 의미의 〈능력〉을 나타내는 「be + able + to-v」가 함께 쓰인 should be able to use는 '사용할 수 있어야 한다'라고 해석된다.

READING 2　The Amazing Cajon

▶ **Reading Comprehension**
1 a　2 (1) F (2) T　3 d　4 acoustic performances

▶ **Grammar Inside Starter**
Check Up 1 I didn't eat pizza yesterday.　2 Did she read the newspaper?

해석　　페루의 카혼은 흥미로운 악기이다. 그것은 상자처럼 생겼고, 연주자들은 그 위에 앉아 손으로 그것을 연주한다! 그것은 단순해 보이지만, 매우 다양한 음색을 만들어 낼 수 있다.
　　카혼의 이야기는 서아프리카에서 시작된다. 서아프리카는 풍부한 드럼 연주와 춤의 전통을 가지고 있다. 노예 제도 시기 동안, 많은 서아프리카인은 붙잡혀서 미대륙으로 끌려갔다. 연안에 위치한 페루에서 아프리카인 노예들은 그들의 전통 드럼 연주가 그리웠지만, 더는 드럼을 갖고 있지 않았다. 이것이 그들로 하여금 드럼을 연주하는 것을 막았을까? 아니다! 그들은 오래된 해상 운송 상자를 많이 가지고 있어서, 그 상자들을 드럼처럼 연주하기로 했다. 그 소리는 인상적이었다!
　　이것이 카혼의 탄생이었다. 후에, 카혼은 스페인 플라멩코 연주자들 사이에서 인기를 얻었고 결국 재즈, 블루스, 그리고 록으로 퍼졌다. 오늘날, 카혼은 많은 종류의 현대 음악에서 사용되고, 특히 전자 장치를 쓰지 않는 공연에서 인기가 있다.

어휘　amazing 형 놀라운, 굉장한　Peruvian 형 페루의　instrument 명 기구; *악기 (percussion instrument 타악기)　produce 동 만들어 내다　a range of 다양한　tone 명 어조, 말투; *음색, 음조　begin 동 시작되다, 시작하다　rich 형 부유한; *풍부한　tradition 명 전통 (traditional 형 전통의)　slavery 명 노예; *노예 제도 (slave 명 노예)　capture 동 붙잡다, 포획하다　coastal 형 연안[해안]의　miss 동 그리워하다　not ~ anymore 더는 ~이 아닌[하지 않는]　impressive 형 인상적인, 감명 깊은　birth 명 탄생, 출생　eventually 부 결국　spread 동 펼치다; *퍼지다, 확산되다　nowadays 부 오늘날에는　acoustic 형 전자 장치를 쓰지 않는　performance 명 공연　[문제] plenty of 많은　shipping 명 해상 운송　crate 명 상자

구문　1행 ..., and players [sit on it] **and** [play it with their hands]!
→ 등위접속사 and로 sit on it과 play it with their hands가 대등하게 연결되어 있다.

5행 ..., many West Africans **were captured** *and* **brought** to the Americas.
→ were captured와 (were) brought는 「be + v-ed」의 수동태로, '~되었다'의 의미이다.
→ 등위접속사 and로 were captured와 (were) brought 이하가 대등하게 연결되어 있다.

8행 Did this **stop them from drumming**?
→ 「stop + 목적어 + from + v-ing」는 '~가 …하는 것을 막다'라는 의미이다.

9행 They had plenty of old shipping crates, so they **decided to play** the crates like drums.
→ 동사 decide는 to부정사(to play)를 목적어로 취하며, '~하기로 (결심)하다'라는 의미이다.

10행 Later, the cajon [became popular among Spanish flamenco players] **and** [eventually spread to jazz, blues, and rock].

→ 등위접속사 and로 became ... players와 eventually spread 이하가 대등하게 연결되어 있다.

Check Up   **1** spread   **2** similar   **3** hollow   **4** capture   **5** tradition   **6** performance   **7** modern   **8** impressive

---

UNIT 02 | Economics

pp. 13–18

READING 1   The Framing Effect

▶ **Reading Comprehension**

1 d   **2** b   **3** (1) facts about their products sound better (2) the prices of their products seem lower   **4** a

▶ **Grammar Inside Starter**

Check Up   **1** soft   **2** bad

해석   당신이 감기에 걸렸다고 상상해 보아라. 당신은 조금의 약을 사고 싶다. 한 약은 그것이 90%의 성공률이 있다고 한다. 다른 것은 그것이 매 10명 중 한 명에게는 도움이 되지 않는다고 한다. 당신은 어느 것을 고를 것인가?

둘은 정확히 똑같은 성공률을 가지고 있다. 정보가 그저 다른 방식으로 제시된 것뿐이다. 하지만 대부분 사람들은 첫 번째 약을 고를 것이다. 이것은 '프레이밍 효과'라고 불린다. 프레이밍 효과는 '무엇을 말하는가'에 대한 것이 아니라, '그것을 어떻게 말하는가'에 대한 것이다. 이는 소비자의 결정에 강력한 영향을 미칠 수 있다.

프레이밍 효과는 광고에서 흔히 발견된다. 마케팅 담당자들은 그들의 상품에 대한 사실이 더 좋게 들리게 하려고 그것을 사용한다. 그들은 또한 그들의 상품 가격이 더 낮아 보이게 하려고 프레이밍 효과를 사용한다. 일 년에 350달러인 회원권은 너무 비싸게 들릴지도 모른다. 하지만 '하루에 1달러 미만'은 어떤가? 그것은 훨씬 더 저렴하게 들린다!

그러니, 다음에 무언가를 살 때, 프레이밍 효과에 속지 마라!

어휘   effect 몡 효과; 영향   imagine 동 상상하다   have a cold 감기에 걸리다   medicine 몡 약, 약물   success 몡 성공   rate 몡 비율, ~율   out of ~ 밖으로; *~ 중에(서)   every 혱 모든; *매 ~, ~마다   choose 동 고르다, 선택하다   exactly 뿐 정확히   present 동 제시[제출]하다   have an effect on ~에 영향을 미치다   consumer 몡 소비자   decision 몡 결정, 판단   commonly 뿐 흔히, 보통   advertising 몡 광고 (advertisement 몡 광고)   marketer 몡 마케팅 담당자   fact 몡 사실   product 몡 상품, 제품   price 몡 가격   seem 동 ~해 보이다, ~인 것 같다   low 혱 낮은   membership 몡 회원권   cost 동 (값·비용이) ~이다   expensive 혱 비싼, 돈이 많이 드는   cheap 혱 저렴한, 돈이 적게 드는   fool 동 속이다   [문제] reasonable 혱 적정한, 너무 비싸지 않은   satisfied 혱 만족한

구문   **1행** One says [it has a 90% success rate].

→ [ ]는 동사 says의 목적어 역할을 하는 명사절로, 앞에 접속사 that이 생략되어 있다.

6행 The framing effect is not about "[what you say]"; it is about "[how you say it]."
→ [ ]는 모두 전치사 about의 목적어로 쓰인 간접의문문으로, 「의문사 + 주어 + 동사 ~」의 어순을 따른다.

9행 Marketers use it **to make** facts about their products sound better.
→ to make 이하는 '~을 만들기 위해'의 의미로, 〈목적〉을 나타내는 부사적 용법의 to부정사구이다.
→ 「make + 목적어 + 동사원형」은 '~가 …하게 하다'의 의미이다. 사역동사 make는 목적격 보어로 동사원형 (sound)을 쓴다.

12행 A membership [that costs $350 a year] might sound too expensive.
→ [ ]는 선행사 a membership을 수식하는 주격 관계대명사절이다.

13행 It sounds **much** cheaper!
→ much는 비교급 cheaper를 강조하는 부사로, '훨씬'의 의미이다.

14행 So, **next time you buy** something, *don't* **be fooled by** the framing effect!
→ 「next time + 주어 + 동사」는 '다음에 ~가 …할 때'라는 의미이다.
→ 「don't + 동사원형」으로 시작하는 문장은 '~하지 마라'라는 의미의 명령문이다.
→ 「be + v-ed + by」 형태의 수동태는 '~에 의해 …되다'라는 의미이다.

READING 2　A Servant's Dream

▶ **Reading Comprehension**
1 d　2 d　3 b　4 sold the right to use the name of her salon

▶ **Grammar Inside Starter**
Check Up 1 angry　2 him a genius

해석　　Martha Harper는 큰 야망을 품은 캐나다인 가정부였다. 그녀는 자기 자신의 사업을 위한 돈을 모으려고 25년 동안 일했다. 1888년에, 그녀는 최초의 대중 미용실인 Harper's Salon을 개업했다.

그 당시, 대부분 여자들은 집에서 직접 머리를 손질했다. 미용실에서 머리를 하는 것은 획기적인 생각이었다! 이것이 Martha의 미용실을 크게 성공하게 했다. 그녀의 고객들은 Martha가 다른 도시에 더 많은 미용실을 열도록 권했다. 하지만 Martha는 자신을 대신해서 그녀의 가게를 운영할 종업원을 고용하고 싶지 않았다. 그래서 그녀는 다른 사업 모델을 내놓았다.

1891년에, Martha는 다른 여성들에게 자신의 미용실 이름을 사용할 권리를 팔았다. Martha에게서 보수를 받는 대신, 그 여성들은 그들 자신의 Harper's Salon을 운영했다! 이 방법은 후에 '가맹업'으로 알려지게 되었다. 1920년대에는, 이 미용실이 전 세계에 걸쳐 500개가 넘게 있었다!

오늘날, Martha의 가맹 사업 모델은 널리 사용되고 있다. 이 선구적인 여성 사업가는 맥도날드와 같은 대규모 글로벌 사업의 확산을 가능하게 했다.

어휘　servant 몡 하인, 고용인　household 몡 가정의　ambition 몡 야망, 포부　business 몡 사업　public 몡 대중의　hairdressing salon 미용실　do hair 머리를 손질하다　innovative 몡 획기[혁신]적인　huge 몡 매우 큰, 거대한　success 몡 성공한 것, 성공작　hire 통 고용하다　employee 몡 종업원, 직원　run 통 달리다; *운영하다　on one's behalf ~을 대신하여　come up with ~을 내놓다[제안하다]　right 몡 옳은 일; *권리, 권한　pay 통 (일의 대가 등을) 지불하다　method 몡 방법　later 면 후[뒤]에　franchising 몡 가맹업　worldwide 면 전 세계에

걸쳐   **widely** ⊕ 널리, 폭넓게   **pioneering** ⊚ 선구적인 (**pioneer** ⊚ 선구자)   **businesswoman** ⊚ 여성 사업가
spread ⊚ 확산, 전파   **global** ⊚ 세계적인   [문제] **customer** ⊚ 고객, 손님   **encourage** ⊚ 격려하다; *권하다, 장려하다

구문

3행 She worked for 25 years **to save** money for her own business.
→ to save 이하는 '~을 모으기 위해'의 의미로, 〈목적〉을 나타내는 부사적 용법의 to부정사구이다.

8행 This **made Martha's salon a huge success**.
→ 「make + 목적어 + 명사」는 '~을 …로 만들다'의 의미이다. 동사 make의 목적격 보어로 명사구 a huge success가 쓰였다.

9행 Her customers **encouraged Martha to open** more salons in other cities.
→ 「encourage + 목적어 + to-v」는 '~에게 …할 것을 권하다[장려하다]'라는 의미이다. 동사 encouraged의 목적격 보어로 to부정사구인 to open 이하가 쓰였다.

9행 But Martha didn't **want to hire** employees *to run* her shops on her behalf.
→ 동사 want는 목적어로 to부정사(to hire 이하)를 취한다.
→ to run 이하는 형용사적 용법의 to부정사구로, 명사 employees를 수식한다.

12행 In 1891, Martha sold the right **to use** the name of her salon to other women.
→ to use 이하는 형용사적 용법의 to부정사구로, 명사 the right를 수식한다.

13행 **Instead of** *being paid* by Martha, the women ran their own Harper's Salons!
→ instead of는 '~ 대신(에)'이라는 의미의 전치사로, 뒤에 명사 상당어구가 온다.
→ being paid는 '보수를 받는 것'이라는 의미로, 동명사의 수동태이다.

14행 This method later **became known as** "franchising."
→ become known as는 '~로 알려지게 되다'라는 의미이다.

16행 This pioneering businesswoman **made the spread of huge global businesses such as McDonald's possible**.
→ 「make + 목적어 + 형용사」는 '~을 …하게 하다'의 의미이다. 동사 made의 목적격 보어로 형용사 possible이 쓰였다.

● **VOCABULARY INSIDE**

Check Up   1 run   2 cost   3 ambition   4 decision   5 household   6 global
7 success   8 hire

▶ **Reading Comprehension**
　1 c　2 c　3 keep a safe distance between one another　4 a

▶ **Grammar Inside Starter**
　Check Up　I sent him a Christmas card

해석　　비행기 한 대가 뉴욕에서 이륙하여 런던에 착륙한다. 조종사는 무사히 비행을 완료했지만, 그가 그것을 혼자 해낸 것은 아니다. 안전한 여행을 하기 위해서는 많은 사람들이 필요하다.

　　한 가지 중요한 직업은 항공 운항 관제사이다. 항공 운항 관제사는 항공기와 무선 및 레이더 연락을 지속하며 조종사에게 기상 상태와 같은 정보를 제공한다. 하지만 더 복잡한 임무들도 있다. 바쁜 기간에는, 매시간 수많은 항공기가 있을 수 있다. 그래서 항공 운항 관제사들은 반드시 비행기들이 서로 안전거리를 유지하도록 한다.

　　조종사는 한 번에 한 대의 항공기를 책임지지만, 항공 운항 관제사는 동시에 많은 항공기들을 다뤄야 한다. 예를 들어, 항공 운항 관제사는 다른 항공기에 그 지역의 기상 정보를 말하는 동안 한 항공기가 착륙하는 것을 도울 수 있다. 또한, 항공 운항 관제사는 신속하게 결정을 내려서 응급 상황이나 예상치 못한 일에 준비되어야 한다.

어휘　plane 명 비행기　take off 이륙하다　land 동 착륙하다, 내려앉다　pilot 명 조종사, 비행사　complete 동 완료하다, 끝마치다　flight 명 비행, 여행; 항공기　safely 부 무사히, 안전하게　alone 부 혼자　journey 명 여행, 이동　radio 명 라디오; *무선 (통신)　contact 명 연락　aircraft 명 항공기　conditions 명 (날씨 등의) 상태　complicated 형 복잡한　duty 명 의무; *임무, 직무　as well ~도, 또한, 역시　thousands of 수천의; *수많은　every 형 모든; *매 ~, ~마다　distance 명 거리　one another 서로　responsible 형 책임이 있는　at a time 한 번에　handle 동 다루다, 처리하다　at the same 동시에　decision 명 결정, 판단　quickly 부 신속하게, 빨리　prepared 형 준비된　emergency 명 응급 (상황)　unexpected 형 예상치 못한, 예상 밖의

구문　　**2행**　Many people **are needed** *to make* a safe journey.
　→ are needed는 「be + v-ed」 형태의 수동태이다.
　→ to make 이하는 '~을 만들기 위해'의 뜻으로, 〈목적〉을 나타내는 부사적 용법의 to부정사구이다.

　8행　So air traffic controllers **make sure that the planes keep** a safe distance ... .
　→ 「make sure (that) + 주어 + 동사」는 '반드시 ~가 …하게 하다', '~가 …할 것을 확실히 하다'라는 의미이다.

　10행　**While** a pilot is responsible for one flight at a time, an air traffic controller ... .
　→ 접속사 while은 〈대조〉를 나타내어 '~하지만', '~하는 반면'이라는 의미이다.
　→ 「be + responsible for」는 '~을 책임지다'라는 의미이다.

　11행　For instance, an air traffic controller might **help one aircraft land** while he *tells another aircraft the weather report* ... .
　→ 「help + 목적어 + 동사원형」은 '~가 …하는 것을 돕다'라는 의미이다. 동사 help의 목적격 보어로 동사원형 land가 쓰였다.
　→ 「tell + 간접목적어 + 직접목적어」는 '~에게 …을 말해주다'라는 의미이다.

▶ **Reading Comprehension**

1 a　2 (C) → (A) → (B)　3 temperature, humidity, lighting　4 b

▶ **Grammar Inside Level 1**

Check Up Tom advised me to read

해석　어떻게 좋은 얼음은 스케이트 선수들이 더 잘 경기하게 할까요? 오늘, 빙상 기술자 Ralph Lewis가 우리에게 말해주기 위해 오셨습니다.

Q: 빙상 기술자로서 어떤 일을 하시나요?

A: 저는 아이스링크를 관리하고 있습니다. 먼저, 저는 콘크리트를 차갑게 하고 얼음을 층층이 쌓기 위해 조심히 그 위에 물을 뿌립니다. 그런 다음 기계로 먼지를 제거합니다. 마지막으로, 아이스링크의 온도, 습도, 조명을 확인하는데, 그것들이 얼음에 영향을 미치기 때문입니다.

Q: 당신의 직업에서 중요한 것은 무엇인가요?

A: 스포츠마다 얼음의 온도와 두께를 조절하는 것이 중요합니다. 스피드 스케이팅 선수들은 얼음 위에서 세게 발을 내디디고 빠르게 회전합니다. 더 얇고 더 차가운 얼음은 그들이 이것을 할 수 있게 해줍니다. 하지만, 피겨 스케이팅 선수들은 그런 얼음 위에서 점프하면 다칠 것입니다. 그들에게는, 얼음이 더 두껍고 덜 차가워야 합니다.

Q: 당신의 직업에 대해 말하고 싶은 것이 있나요?

A: 좋은 얼음은 선수들이 안전하고 능숙하게 경기할 수 있게 합니다. 저는 그것을 위해 열심히 일합니다.

어휘　technician 몡 기술자　skater 몡 스케이트 선수　perform 통 수행하다; *(경기 등을) 하다　take care of ~을 관리하다[돌보다]　ice rink 아이스링크　cool 혱 시원한; *차갑게 하다　concrete 몡 콘크리트　carefully 뷔 조심히　spray 통 뿌리다　layer 몡 층, 겹; 통 *층층이 쌓다　remove 통 제거하다　dust 몡 먼지　temperature 몡 온도　humidity 몡 습도　lighting 몡 조명　affect 통 영향을 미치다　step 통 발을 내디디다　hard 뷔 세게; 열심히　thin 혱 얇은　hurt 통 다치게 하다　thick 혱 두꺼운　enable 통 할 수 있게 하다　athlete 몡 운동선수　safely 뷔 안전하게　skillfully 뷔 능숙하게, 솜씨 있게　[문제] adjust 통 조절하다　maintain 통 유지하다

구문　**2행** Today, ice technician Ralph Lewis is here **to tell us**.

→ to tell us는 '우리에게 말해주기 위해'의 뜻으로, 〈목적〉을 나타내는 부사적 용법의 to부정사구이다.

7행 Finally, I check the rink's temperature, humidity, and lighting, **as** they affect the ice.

→ 접속사 as는 〈이유〉를 나타내며, '~이기 때문에'라는 의미이다.

10행 It's important **to adjust** the ice's temperature and thickness for each sport.

→ it은 가주어이고 to adjust 이하는 진주어이다.

11행 Thinner and colder ice **allows them to do** this.

→ 「allow + 목적어 + to-v」는 '~가 …할 수 있게 하다'라는 뜻이다. 동사 allow의 목적격 보어로 to do 이하가 쓰였다.

12행 However, figure skaters **would** hurt *themselves* **from** jumping on that ice.

→ 조동사 would는 〈확실한 추측〉을 나타내며, '~할 것이다'라는 의미이다.

→ 재귀대명사 themselves는 '그들 자신'이라는 의미이다. 재귀대명사는 행위(hurt)의 주체(figure skaters)와 행위의 대상이 동일할 때 쓰인다.

→ 이 문장에서 전치사 from은 〈원인〉 및 〈이유〉를 나타내며, '~로 인해', '~ 때문에'라는 의미로 쓰였다.

UNIT 04 | Technology

pp. 25–30

READING 1   Smart Bins

▶ **Reading Comprehension**
1 d   2 c   3 d   4 free digital information

▶ **Grammar Inside Starter**
Check Up 1 fix   2 can

해석

새로운 무언가가 도시의 거리로 오고 있다. 싱가포르와 뉴욕에서, 당신은 이미 이것을 많은 거리의 모퉁이에서 볼 수 있다. 그것은 최첨단 쓰레기통인 '스마트 쓰레기통'이다.

스마트 쓰레기통은 여러 방면으로 동네를 더 좋게 만든다. 태양열 기술을 이용하여, 그것은 쓰레기를 눌러 부순다. 이 방식으로, 그것은 더 많은 쓰레기를 담을 수 있다. 그리고 그것이 가득 차면 특수 감지기가 쓰레기 수거팀에게 알려준다.

가장 놀라운 것은 각각의 스마트 쓰레기통이 와이파이 핫스팟이라는 점이다. 도시들은 수많은 사람들에게 강한 신호를 보내기 위해 도시 거리의 모퉁이마다 스마트 쓰레기통을 둘 수 있다. 무엇보다도, 와이파이는 사용자들에게 완전히 무료이다. 많은 사람들은 매일 인터넷을 사용하는 것을 즐기지만, 일부 사람들은 인터넷 접속을 위한 비용을 지불할 형편이 안 된다는 것을 종종 잊는다. 하지만 스마트 쓰레기통은 무료의 디지털 정보를 그 구역의 모든 사람들에게 가져다준다. 게다가, 그것들은 환경친화적이다. 그것들은 똑똑하지 않은가?

어휘 bin 몡 (쓰레기)통   street 몡 거리   already 분 이미, 벌써   corner 몡 모퉁이   high-tech 혱 최첨단의   trash can 쓰레기통   neighborhood 몡 동네, 이웃   several 혱 여러, 몇몇의   crush 동 눌러 부수다, 찌부러뜨리다   sensor 몡 센서, 감지기   collection 몡 수집품; *수거, 수집   place 동 두다, 놓다   give out (소리·빛·냄새 등)을 내다[발하다]   signal 몡 신호   totally 분 완전히, 전적으로   free 혱 자유로운; *무료의   afford to ~할 형편이 되다   access 몡 접근; *접속   area 몡 구역, 장소   eco-friendly 혱 친환경적인   [문제] policy 몡 정책   equal 혱 동일한   empty 혱 텅 빈; 동 *비우다

구문 1행 **Something new** is coming to city streets.
→ -thing으로 끝나는 대명사는 뒤에서 형용사(new)의 수식을 받는다.

4행 A smart bin **makes a neighborhood better** in several ways.
→ 「make + 목적어 + 형용사」는 '~을 …하게 만들다'라는 의미이다. 동사 make의 목적격 보어로 형용사 good의 비교급 better가 쓰였다.

8행 The most amazing thing is [that each smart bin is a Wi-Fi hotspot].

→ [ ]는 동사 is의 보어 역할을 하는 명사절이다.

9행 ... on every street corner **to give out** a strong signal to thousands of people.
→ to give out 이하는 '~을 보내기 위해'의 뜻으로, 〈목적〉을 나타내는 부사적 용법의 to부정사구이다.

11행 Many people **enjoy using** the internet every day, but they often forget [that some people cannot ...].
→ 동사 enjoy는 목적어로 동명사(using 이하)를 취한다.
→ [ ]는 동사 forget의 목적어 역할을 하는 명사절이다.

14행 **Aren't** they smart?
→ 부정형(aren't)으로 시작하는 부정 의문문으로, '~이지 않은가?'로 해석한다.

READING 2　Weather Forecasts

▶ **Reading Comprehension**
1 d　2 forecast　3 d　4 compare the results with previous weather patterns

▶ **Grammar Inside Starter**
Check Up don't have to

해석　　당신은 신발을 신고 책가방을 챙긴다. 나가려고 문을 연 바로 그 때, 당신의 엄마는 "우산을 가져가야 해. 오늘 비가 올 거야."라고 말한다. 그녀는 미래를 들여다볼 수 있을까? 아니다! 그녀는 단지 일기 예보를 확인한 것이다.
　　일기 예보는 우리에게 날씨에 대한 예측을 제공한다. 그것들은 우리가 입을 옷에 대한 결정을 내리는 데 도움을 줄 수 있다. 그리고 그것들은 또한 위험한 기상 상황이 예상되면 우리에게 경고할 수 있다.
　　일기 예보는 기상학자라고 불리는 사람들에 의해 만들어진다. 정확한 예측을 하기 위해서, 그들은 고도로 발달한 기상 관측소에서 나온 수많은 양의 정보를 이용해야 한다. 이 기상 관측소들은 많은 곳으로부터 정보를 수집한다. 예를 들어, 그것들은 배와 비행기에 달린 특수한 기구로부터 자료를 얻는다. 기상 풍선과 인공위성도 그것들에 자료를 보낸다.
　　이 자료를 처리하기 위해, 기상학자들은 슈퍼컴퓨터를 사용해야 한다. 그런 다음, 그들은 결과를 이전의 날씨 패턴에 비교하여 예측할 수 있다.

어휘　weather 명 날씨　forecast 명 예보, 예측　put on ~을 입다[신다]　grab 동 붙잡다, 움켜잡다　see into ~을 들여다보다　prediction 명 예측 (predict 동 예측하다)　decision 명 결정, 판단　warn 동 경고하다　dangerous 형 위험한　conditions 명 (특정 시기의 날씨) 상황　expect 동 예상하다　create 동 만들다, 창조하다　accurate 형 정확한　tons of 수많은　information 명 정보　highly 부 고도로, 매우　advanced 형 발달[진보]한 (advance 명 발전)　weather station 기상 관측소　collect 동 수집하다　for example 예를 들어　data 명 자료, 데이터　instrument 명 기구　process 동 처리하다　compare 동 비교하다　result 명 결과　previous 형 이전의　pattern 명 패턴, 양식　[문제] satellite 명 인공위성

구문　1행 Just **as** you open the door *to leave*, your mom says, ...
→ 접속사 as는 〈시간〉을 나타내어 '~할 때'라는 의미이다.
→ to leave는 〈목적〉을 나타내며, '나가기 위해'라는 의미의 부사적 용법의 to부정사이다.

2행 It's **going to rain** today.
→ 「be + going + to-v」는 '~할 것[예정]이다'라는 의미로, 미래 시제를 나타낸다.

They can **help us make** decisions about the clothes [we wear].
→ 「help + 목적어 + 동사원형」은 '~가 …하는 것을 도와주다'라는 뜻이다. 동사 help의 목적격 보어로 동사원형 make가 쓰였다.
→ [ ]는 선행사 the clothes를 수식하는 관계대명사절로, 앞에 목적격 관계대명사 that[which]이 생략되었다.

8행 Weather forecasts **are created** by people *called meteorologists*.
→ are created는 「be + v-ed」의 형태의 수동태이다.
→ called meteorologists는 명사 people을 수식하는 과거분사구이다.

14행 Then they can **compare** the results **with** previous weather patterns *to make* ... .
→ compare A with B는 'A를 B에 비교하다'라는 의미이다.
→ to make 이하는 〈결과〉를 나타내는 부사적 용법의 to부정사구이다.

● **VOCABULARY INSIDE**

Check Up 1 afford 2 crush 3 compare 4 result 5 grab 6 neighborhood
7 accurate 8 access

UNIT 05 | Solutions
pp. 31–36

READING 1 Green Billboards

▶ **Reading Comprehension**
1 d 2 (1) desert, little water (2) Air pollution, heavy traffic 3 b 4 a

▶ **Grammar Inside Starter**
Check Up 1 is smiling 2 are standing

해석   페루의 수도인, 리마에서의 삶은 쉽지 않다. 그 도시는 사막에 있어서, 물이 거의 없다. 또한, 극심한 교통량으로 대기 오염 물질이 증가하고 있다. 하지만 한 지역 대학이 이러한 문제에 맞서 싸우기 위해 독특한 무기를 만들었는데, 바로 광고판이다.
그 대학교는 두 가지 유형의 광고판을 만들었다. 첫 번째 유형은 공기로부터 수분을 흡수하고 그것을 정화한다. 그런 다음 그것은 광고판 아래에 있는 탱크에 물을 저장한다. 목이 마른 사람들은 수도꼭지에서 물을 마실 수 있다. 그 광고판은 매일 90리터가 넘는 물을 모은다.
두 번째 유형의 광고판은 공기를 여과한다. 그것은 더러운 공기를 흡수해서, 오염 물질을 제거하고, 그런 다음 대기 중으로 깨끗한 공기를 내보낸다. 각 광고판은 약 다섯 개의 도시 구획의 공기를 정화할 수 있다.
물론, 그 광고판은 여전히 광고로 사용된다. 그러나 이 광고판으로, 그 대학은 학교의 좋은 이미지를 보여 주면서, 동시에 깨끗한 공기와 물을 제공하고 있다!

어휘   billboard 명 (옥외의 커다란) 광고[게시]판 capital 명 수도 desert 명 사막 pollution 명 오염 (물질) increase

⑧ 증가하다, 늘다   due to ～ 때문에   heavy ⑱ 무거운; *극심한   traffic ⑲ 교통(량), 차량들   local ⑱ 지역[현지]의   create ⑧ 만들다   unusual ⑱ 독특한, 흔치 않은   weapon ⑲ 무기   absorb ⑧ 흡수하다, 빨아들이다   purify ⑧ 정화하다   thirsty ⑱ 목이 마른, 갈증이 난   tap ⑲ 수도꼭지   collect ⑧ 모으다   take in ～을 흡수하다   remove ⑧ 제거하다   release ⑧ 내보내다, 방출하다   atmosphere ⑲ 대기   city block (도시의) 구획   advertisement ⑲ 광고 (advertising ⑲ 광고)   present ⑧ 보여 주다, 나타내다   provide ⑧ 제공[공급]하다   [문제] store ⑧ 저장[보관]하다   below ⑳ ～ 아래에   sign ⑲ 표지판, 간판   filter ⑧ 여과하다, 거르다

구문

2행 The city **is located in** a desert, so it has *little water*.
→ 「be + located in ～」은 '～에 있다'라는 의미이다.
→ 수량 형용사 little은 '거의 없는'이란 뜻이며, 셀 수 없는 명사(water) 앞에 쓰인다.

5행 But a local university **has created** an unusual weapon *to fight these problems*: … .
→ has created는 「have/has + v-ed」 형태의 현재완료로, 이 문장에서는 〈완료〉를 의미한다.
→ to fight these problems는 '이러한 문제에 맞서 싸우기 위해'라는 뜻으로, 〈목적〉을 나타내는 부사적 용법의 to부정사구이다.

17행 Of course, the billboards **are** still **used** *as* advertisements.
→ are used는 「be + v-ed」 형태의 수동태로, '사용되다'의 의미이다.
→ 전치사 as는 〈수단〉을 나타내며, 이 문장에서는 '～로써'의 의미로 쓰였다.

17행 …, the university [**is presenting** a good image of their school], *and* [**providing** …]!
→ is presenting과 (is) providing은 「be + v-ing」 형태의 현재진행형으로, 각각 '나타내고 있다'와 '제공하고 있다'의 의미이다.
→ 등위접속사 and로 is presenting … school과 (is) providing 이하가 대등하게 연결되어 있다.

READING 2   The Seabin Project

▶ **Reading Comprehension**
1 b   2 d   3 a, b   4 Attaching a special filter to the Seabin

▶ **Grammar Inside Level 1**
Check Up designing

해석   Seabin은 물에 떠 있는 쓰레기통이다. 그것은 바다에서 쓰레기를 제거하기 위해 호주의 서퍼들에 의해 발명되었다. 일단 설치되면, 그것은 자력으로 쓰레기를 모으고 하루 종일 작동할 수 있다!

Seabin은 재활용된 플라스틱으로 만들어진다. 그리고 그것은 천연 재료로 만들어진 그물 주머니를 내부에 가지고 있다. 바닷물은 펌프로 그물망에 관통하여 빨아들여진 다음, 바다로 다시 방출된다. 하지만 물속에 있던 쓰레기는 주머니에 걸려 Seabin 안에 있게 된다. 또한 Seabin에 특별한 여과기를 부착하는 것은 그것이 물에서 기름을 제거하는 것을 가능하게 할 것이다! 이 놀라운 시스템은 바다에서 매일 3.9킬로그램의 오염 물질을 제거할 수 있다.

펌프가 필요하기 때문에, Seabin을 바다 한 가운데에서 사용하는 것은 가능하지 않다. 그래서, 당신은 그것이 육지 가까이에서 사용되는 것만 볼 것이다. 하지만 그것은 부두와 항구 주변의 물을 깨끗하게 하는 데 매우 효과적이다.

어휘   float ⑧ (물에) 뜨다   garbage ⑲ 쓰레기   invent ⑧ 발명하다 (invention ⑲ 발명)   surfer ⑲ 서퍼(파도 타기 하는 사람)   remove ⑧ 제거하다   trash ⑲ 쓰레기   ocean ⑲ 바다, 대양   once ⑳ 일단 ～하면   set up 설치하다

collect ⑧ 모으다   by oneself 자력으로, 도움을 받지 않고   run ⑧ 달리다; *작동하다   recycle ⑧ 재활용하다   mesh ⑲ 그물(망)   inside ⑨ 안에, 내부에; ⑳ ~ 안에   made of ~로 만들어진   natural ⑬ 천연[자연]의   material ⑲ 직물, 천; *재료   suck ⑧ 빨아들이다, 흡수하다   through ⑳ ~을 관통하여   release ⑧ 풀어주다; *방출하다   attach ⑧ 붙이다   filter ⑧ 여과하다; ⑲ *여과기   allow ⑧ 허락하다, ~하게 해주다   amazing ⑬ 놀라운, 굉장한   pollution ⑲ 오염 (물질)   possible ⑬ 가능한   near ⑳ ~ 가까이에   land ⑲ 육지, 땅   effective ⑬ 효과적인   dock ⑲ 부두   harbor ⑲ 항구   [문제] prevent ⑧ 예방[방지]하다   device ⑲ 장치

구문   **1행** The Seabin is a **floating** garbage bin.
  → floating은 명사구 garbage bin을 수식하는 현재분사이다.

  2행 It **was invented by** Australian surfers *to remove* trash from the ocean.
  → was invented by는 「be + v-ed + by」 형태의 수동태로, '~에 의해 발명되었다'의 의미이다.
  → to remove 이하는 '~을 없애기 위해'라는 뜻으로, 〈목적〉을 나타내는 부사적 용법의 to부정사구이다.

  7행 And it has a mesh bag inside [made of natural materials].
  → [ ]는 명사구 a mesh bag을 수식하는 과거분사구이다.

  10행 [Attaching a special filter to the Seabin] will also *allow it to remove* oil from the water!
  → [ ]는 문장의 주어 역할을 하는 동명사구이다.
  → 「allow + 목적어 + to-v」는 '~가 …하는 것을 가능하게 하다'의 의미이다. 동사 allow는 목적격 보어로 to부정사구 to remove 이하가 쓰였다.

  15행 So, you'll only **see them used** near land.
  → 「see + 목적어 + v-ed」는 '~가 …되는 것을 보다'라는 뜻이다.

  15행 But they are very effective at [cleaning the water around docks and harbors].
  → [ ]는 전치사 at의 목적어 역할을 하는 동명사구이다.

● **VOCABULARY INSIDE**

Check Up   **1** effective   **2** attach   **3** recycle   **4** pollution   **5** desert   **6** unusual
     7 possible   **8** purify

UNIT 06 | Cooperation
pp. 37-42

READING 1   **Cooperating for Honey**

▶ **Reading Comprehension**
  1 d   **2** the eggs, larvae, and beeswax in bee nests   **3** d   **4** (1) F (2) T (3) F (4) T

해석   어떤 동물들은 다른 동물들과 특별한 관계를 맺는 것으로부터 이익을 얻는다. 하지만 당신은 인간과 새와의 관계에 대해 들어본 적이 있는가?

    꿀잡이새라고 불리는 새들은 인간과 함께 일한다. 그들의 이름이 암시하는 것처럼, 그들은 사람들을 꿀로 안내한다. 그들의 주요 먹이는 벌집에 있는 알, 유충, 그리고 밀랍이다. 하지만 부수어서 열기에 어려운 것들도 있다. 이러한 경우에, 꿀잡이새들은 인간과 함께 일해야 한다.

    (C) 꿀잡이새가 벌집을 발견하면, 그것은 근처의 인간들을 향해 울음소리를 낸다. (B) 인간들은 그 소리에 답한 다음 그것을 따라간다. (A) 벌집에서, 인간들은 연기를 사용해서 벌을 진정시킨다. 그러고 나서 그들은 벌집을 부수고 꿀을 가져간다. 꿀잡이새는 남은 음식을 먹는다.

    탄자니아의 Hadza족은 꿀잡이새와 협력하는 사람들의 좋은 예이다. 그 새들 덕분에, 그들의 식이의 약 10퍼센트가 꿀이다!

어휘   **cooperate** ⑧ 협력하다   **honey** ⑲ 꿀   **benefit** ⑲ 혜택, 이득; ⑧ *이익을 얻다   **relationship** ⑲ 관계   **human** ⑲ 인간   **like** ⑳ ~처럼; ㉚ *~하는 것처럼, ~하듯이   **suggest** ⑧ 제안하다; *암시[시사]하다   **guide** ⑧ 안내하다   **bee nest** 벌집   **case** ⑲ 경우   **smoke** ⑲ 연기   **calm** ⑧ 진정시키다   **return** ⑧ 돌려주다; *대답하다   **call** ⑲ (새·동물의) 울음소리   **follow** ⑧ 따라가다   **call out** ~을 부르다   **nearby** ⑱ 인근의, 가까운 곳의   **leftover** ⑱ 남은   **example** ⑲ 예(시)   **diet** ⑲ 식이, 식단   **thanks to** ~ 덕분에   [문제] **make a living** 살아가다, 생계를 유지하다

구문   **1행** Some animals benefit from [having a special relationship with other animals].
→ [ ]는 전치사 from의 목적어로 쓰인 동명사구이다.

2행 But **have** you ever **heard** of one between humans and birds?
→ have ... heard는 「have/has + v-ed」 형태의 현재완료로, '~한 적 있다'라는 의미의 〈경험〉을 나타낸다.

3행 Birds [called honeyguides] work with humans.
→ [ ]은 명사 birds를 수식하는 과거분사구이다.

5행 But there are **ones** [that are hard **to break open**].
→ 대명사 ones는 앞 문장에서 언급한 명사구 bee nests를 가리킨다.
→ [ ]는 선행사 ones를 수식하는 주격 관계대명사절이다.
→ to break open은 형용사 hard를 수식하는 부사적 용법의 to부정사구이다.

8행 The humans [return the call] **and** then [follow *it*].
→ 등위접속사 and로 return the call과 follow it이 대등하게 연결되어 있다.
→ 인칭대명사 it은 앞에서 언급한 명사 the call을 가리킨다.

9행 **When** a honeyguide finds a bee nest, it calls out to nearby humans.
→ when은 〈시간〉을 나타내는 접속사로 '~할 때에', '~하면'의 의미이다.

12행 ... are a great example of people [who cooperate with honeyguides].
→ [ ]는 선행사 people을 수식하는 주격 관계대명사절이다.

▶ **Reading Comprehension**
1 b　2 a　3 d　4 More than 230 restaurants

▶ **Grammar Inside Level 1**
　Check Up This sweater is as big

해석　　어려움에 처한 누군가를 돕는 것에 항상 추가의 시간이나 돈이 드는 것은 아니다. 그것은 식당에서 식사를 하는 것만큼 간단할 수 있다!

　　　Mealshare라는 이름의 한 자선 단체가 당신으로 하여금 바로 이것을 하게 한다! 참여하기 위해, Mealshare와 파트너인 식당을 방문하라. 그런 다음 메뉴에서 Mealshare 품목을 고르고 당신의 식사를 즐겨라. 그것은 이만큼 쉽다! 이 일이 일어날 때마다, 식당은 Mealshare에 1달러를 기부한다. 당신이 아무런 추가 비용을 지불하지 않고도, 그 돈은 어려움에 처한 누군가에게 식사를 제공하는 데 쓰인다! 그래서 당신은 Mealshare의 슬로건이 말하듯 '하나를 사고 하나를 줄' 수 있다.

　　　Mealshare는 2013년 캐나다에서 경영 대학원 졸업생들에 의해 설립되었다. 그들은 매우 많은 사람들이 제대로 된 식사를 하지 못해 마음이 좋지 않았고, 그래서 식당에 가는 사람들이 타인을 도울 수 있는 편리한 방법을 만들고 싶었다.

　　　그것의 첫 2년 만에, 230개가 넘는 식당이 Mealshare 프로그램에 동참했다. 그리고 그 수는 계속 늘어나고 있다!

어휘　**meal** 명 식사, 끼니　**in need** 어려움에 처한　**cost** 통 (비용·대가가) 들다; 명 비용　**extra** 형 추가의　**simple** 형 간단한, 단순한　**charity** 명 자선 (단체)　**organization** 명 단체, 조직　**exactly** 부 바로, 정확히　**participate** 통 참여[참가]하다　**partner** 명 (사업) 파트너, 동업자　**choose** 통 선택하다, 고르다　**item** 명 품목, 항목　**happen** 통 일어나다, 발생하다　**donate** 통 기부[기증]하다　**slogan** 명 슬로건, 표어　**found** 통 설립하다, 세우다　**business school** 경영 대학원　**graduate** 명 졸업자　**proper** 형 제대로 된, 적절한　**convenient** 형 편리한, 간편한　**restaurant-goer** 명 식당에 가는 사람　**join** 통 함께 하다　**grow** 통 늘어나다, 커지다

구문　**1행** [Helping someone in need] *doesn't always* have to **cost you extra time or money**.
　→ [ ]는 문장의 주어로 쓰인 동명사구이다.
　→ 부정어 not과 부사 always가 함께 쓰이면, '항상 …한 것은 아닌'의 의미로 〈부분 부정〉을 나타낸다.
　→ 「cost + 간접목적어 + 직접목적어」는 '~에게 …의 비용을 지불하게 하다'의 의미이다.

　4행 A charity organization [named Mealshare] *lets you do* exactly this!
　→ [ ]는 명사구 a charity organization을 수식하는 과거분사구이다.
　→ 「let + 목적어 + 동사원형」은 '~가 …하게 하다'라는 의미이다. 사역동사 let은 목적격 보어로 동사원형(do)을 취한다.

　8행 The money **is used to give** a meal to someone in need, *at no extra cost* to you!
　→ 「be used + to-v」는 '~하는 데 사용되다'의 의미이다.
　→ at no extra cost는 '추가의 비용을 지불하지 않고'의 의미이다.

　11행 Mealshare **was founded** in Canada **by** business school graduates in 2013.
　→ was founded by는 「be + v-ed + by」 형태의 수동태이다.

　12행 They were unhappy [that so many people ...], so they wanted to create a convenient way *for restaurant-goers* **to help others**.

→ [ ]는 접속사 that이 이끄는 절로, 감정(unhappy)의 〈원인〉 및 〈이유〉를 설명한다.

→ for restaurant-goers는 to부정사구 to help others의 의미상의 주어이다.

→ to help others는 명사구 a convenient way를 수식하는 형용사적 용법의 to부정사구이다.

16행 And the number **keeps growing**!

→ 「keep + v-ing」는 '계속해서 ~하다'의 의미이다. 동사 keep은 목적어로 동명사(growing)를 취한다.

● VOCABULARY INSIDE

Check Up 1 diet   2 leftover   3 convenient   4 cooperate   5 happen   6 organization
7 relationship   8 donate

UNIT 07 | **Sports**

pp. 43–48

READING 1   On Ice? No, Underwater!

▶ **Reading Comprehension**

1 d   2 d   3 they push the puck into their opponent's goal   4 a

▶ **Grammar Inside Starter**

Check Up nicer than

해석   대부분 사람들은 하키에 대해 생각할 때, 아이스 링크를 상상한다. 하지만 다음에 하키를 하고 싶을 때는, 대신 수영장에 가 봐라. 그곳에서, 당신은 수중에서 하키를 할 수 있다!

수중 하키는 단순한 규칙을 가진 실제 스포츠이다. 참가자들은 오리발과 스노클을 착용한다. 그들은 또한 퍽을 밀어내기 위해 하키용 스틱을 쓰는데, 그 스틱은 아이스하키 스틱보다 더 짧다. 경기 전에, 퍽은 수영장 중앙에 놓인다. 선수들은 자기 팀 골대 위의 벽에 손을 대고 시작 신호를 기다린다. 신호가 울리면, 선수들은 숨을 참고 수영을 한다. 선수들이 상대편의 골대 안으로 퍽을 밀어 넣으면 득점한다. 경기는 15분의 전반과 후반이 있고, 각 팀에는 6명의 선수와 4명의 교체 선수가 있다.

수중 하키는 많은 사람들에게 인기를 쌓고 있다. 이는 그것이 아이스하키나 필드하키보다 더 안전하기 때문이다. 심지어 70대인 선수들이 있다는 것을 들으면 당신은 놀랄지도 모른다!

어휘   underwater ⓟ 물속에서; ⓐ 물속의, 수중의   picture ⓝ 사진, 그림; ⓥ *상상하다   instead ⓟ 대신에   simple ⓐ 단순한, 간단한   rule ⓝ 규칙, 원칙   participant ⓝ 참가자   fin ⓝ 오리발   snorkel ⓝ 스노클(잠수 중 호흡을 위해 사용되는 관)   push ⓥ 밀다   place ⓝ 장소; ⓥ *놓다, 두다   middle ⓝ 중앙, 한가운데   pool ⓝ 수영장   touch ⓥ (손 등으로) 대다, 만지다   above ⓟ ~보다 위에[위로]   goal ⓝ 골대, 골문   signal ⓝ 신호   ring ⓥ (소리가) 울리다   hold one's breath 숨을 참다   score ⓥ 득점하다   opponent ⓝ (대회·논쟁 등의) 상대   half ⓝ (절)반; *(경기의) 전반[후반]   substitute ⓝ 대리자, 대용품; *교체 선수   gain ⓥ (차츰) 쌓다[늘리다]   popularity ⓝ 인기   [문제] the number of ~의 수   require ⓥ 요구하다   equipment ⓝ 기구, 도구

1행 But **next time you want** to play hockey, go to a swimming pool instead.
→ 「next time + 주어 + 동사」는 '다음에 ~가 …할 때'의 의미이다.

5행 They also use hockey sticks **to push the puck**, … .
→ to push the puck은 '퍽을 밀어내기 위해'라는 뜻으로, 〈목적〉을 나타내는 부사적 용법의 to부정사구이다.

6행 Before the game, the puck **is placed** in the middle of the pool.
→ is placed는 「be + v-ed」 형태의 수동태로, '놓이다'의 의미이다.

12행 **This is because** it is *safer than* ice hockey or field hockey.
→ this is because는 '이것은 ~하기 때문이다'의 의미로, 뒤에 〈이유〉 또는 〈원인〉에 해당하는 내용이 온다.
→ safer는 형용사 safe의 비교급으로, 「형용사 비교급 + than」은 '~보다 더 …한'의 의미이다.

13행 You might be surprised **to hear** [that there are even players *in their 70s*]!
→ to hear 이하는 감정(surprised)에 대한 〈이유〉 및 〈원인〉을 나타내는 부사적 용법의 to부정사구이다.
→ [ ]는 to부정사 to hear의 목적어로 쓰인 명사절이다.
→ in one's 70s는 '(~의) 70대에'라는 의미이다.

READING 2   The Trampoline Effect

▶ **Reading Comprehension**
1 d   2 (1) F (2) T   3 c   4 hit too many home runs

▶ **Grammar Inside Starter**
Check Up harder than

캉! 한 야구 선수가 홈런을 친다. 만약 그가 나무 방망이를 사용하면, 공은 약 150미터를 날아갈 것이다. 하지만 만약 그의 방망이가 금속이면, 공은 200미터보다 더 이동할 것이다!

과거에는, 모든 방망이가 나무로 만들어졌다. 나무 방망이는 공을 치면 모양이 바뀌어 버리고 되돌아가지 않는다. 이는 공이 운동 에너지의 일부를 잃게 한다. 그것은 부드러운 잔디 위에서 공이 튀어 오르게 하는 것과 같다. 그것은 아주 높게 튀지 않는다.

하지만 오늘날, 많은 방망이가 알루미늄으로 만들어진다. 알루미늄 방망이는 나무 방망이와 다르게 반응한다. 알루미늄 방망이 역시 공이 그것을 치면 모양이 바뀐다. 하지만 그것은 트램펄린처럼 빠르게 원래의 모양으로 되돌아간다. 이것은 공이 더 멀리 나아가게 한다. 이는 단단한 콘크리트 위에 공을 튀기는 것에 더 가깝다.

하지만 프로 야구 선수들은 경기 중에 나무 방망이를 사용해야 한다. 알루미늄 방망이를 사용하면 그들은 홈런을 너무 많이 치게 된다.

trampoline 명 트램펄린(위에 올라가 점프를 할 수 있는 운동 기구)   effect 명 영향; *효과   hit a home run 홈런을 치다   wooden 형 나무로 된   bat 명 방망이, 배트   metal 명 금속   travel 동 여행하다; *이동하다   past 명 과거   made of ~로 만들어진[구성된]   shape 명 모양, 형태   spring back 튀어 오르다; *(원래의 모양으로) 되돌아가다   cause 동 야기하다, 초래하다   lose 동 잃다   like 전 ~와 같이   bounce 동 (공 등을) 튀게 하다; 튀다   soft 형 부드러운   grass 명 잔디(밭)   react 동 반응하다   hard 형 단단한   concrete 명 콘크리트   professional 형 직업의, 전문적인   during 전 ~ 동안   [문제] advantage 명 이점 (disadvantage 명 약점)   original 형 원래의, 본래의

1행 **If** he **uses** a wooden bat, the ball will fly about 150 meters.
→ 접속사 if가 이끄는 〈조건〉 부사절에서는 현재 시제가 미래 시제를 대신하므로, 동사 uses가 쓰였다.

5행 This **causes the ball to lose** some of its kinetic energy.
→ 「cause + 목적어 + to-v」는 '~가 …하도록 야기하다'라는 의미이다. 동사 cause는 목적격 보어로 to부정사(to lose)를 취한다.

6행 It's like **bouncing** a ball on soft grass.
→ bouncing 이하는 전치사 like의 목적어로 쓰인 동명사구이다.

10행 This **makes the ball go** farther.
→ 「make + 목적어 + 동사원형」은 '~가 …하게 하다'라는 의미이다. 사역동사 make는 목적격 보어로 동사원형 (go)을 취한다.

● VOCABULARY INSIDE

Check Up **1** wooden **2** underwater **3** shape **4** professional **5** react **6** cause
7 gain **8** participants

UNIT 08 | Geography   pp. 49-54

READING 1   South-up Maps

▶ **Reading Comprehension**
1 d **2** d **3** stereotype **4** b

▶ **Grammar Inside Starter**
Check Up It isn't easy to learn a foreign language.

해석

아래에 있는 지도에 대해 어떻게 생각하는가? 그것은 실수인가? 아니다. 사실, 이것은 남쪽이 위에 있는 지도이다.

1979년에, 호주의 한 남성인 Stuart McArthur는 남쪽이 위에 있는 지도를 발행했다. 그의 목표는 사람들이 그의 나라에 대해 다르게 생각하도록 만드는 것이었다. 많은 지도는 유럽, 북미, 혹은 아시아에서 만들어진다. 이런 지도에서 호주는 항상 맨 아랫부분에 있다. McArthur는 '세상의 맨 아래'에 있는 것에 싫증이 났다. 그래서 그는 세상에 새로운 관점을 제시했다.

남쪽이 위에 있는 지도의 또 다른 목표는 사람들이 개발 도상국들에 대해 다르게 생각하도록 돕는 것이다. 지도는 대개 더 부유한 지역을 맨 위에 보여준다. 이는 그 나라들이 '더 가치 있다'는 고정관념을 가중할 수 있다. 몇몇 남쪽이 위에 있는 지도는 아프리카와 남아메리카를 맨 윗부분 가까이에 보여준다. 이는 사람들이 그 나라들의 중요성에 대해 집중할 수 있도록 도와준다.

익숙한 것을 새로운 방식으로 보는 것은 낯설게 느껴지지만, 그것은 우리가 배우도록 돕는다. 당신은 어떻게 지도를 바꾸겠는가?

map 몡 지도   below 뷘 아래에, 밑에   mistake 몡 실수, 잘못   actually 뷘 실제로, 정말로   Australian 톙 호주의, 오스트레일리아의   publish 동 발행[출판]하다 (publisher 몡 발행인)   goal 몡 목표, 목적   differently 뷘 다르게   country 몡 국가, 나라   come from ~에서 나오다[생산되다]   bottom 몡 맨 아래 (부분)   tired of ~에 싫증이 난   perspective 몡 관점, 시각   another 톙 또 다른   developing nation 개발 도상국   rich 톙 부유한   area 몡 지역, 구역   top 몡 맨 위, 윗면   add to ~을 가중하다, ~에 더하다   stereotype 몡 고정관념   focus 동 집중하다   importance 몡 중요성   strange 톙 낯선   familiar 톙 익숙한, 친숙한   [문제] class 몡 반; *계층, 계급   fixed 톙 고정된, 변치 않는   valuable 톙 가치 있는   traditional 톙 전통적인

4행 His goal was to **make people think** differently about his country.
→ 「make + 목적어 + 동사원형」은 '~을 …하게 하다'라는 의미이다. 사역동사 make의 목적격 보어로 동사원형 think가 쓰였다.

6행 McArthur was tired of [being at "the bottom of the world]."
→ [ ]는 전치사 of의 목적어로 쓰인 동명사구이다.

7행 So he **gave the world a new perspective**.
→ 「give + 간접목적어 + 직접목적어」 '~에게 …을 주다'의 의미이다.

8행 Another goal of south-up maps is [to *help people think* differently about developing nations].
→ [ ]는 주격 보어의 역할을 하는 명사적 용법의 to부정사구이다.
→ 「help + 목적어 + 동사원형」은 '~가 …하도록 돕다'라는 의미이다. to부정사 to help의 목적격 보어로 동사원형인 think가 쓰였다.

10행 This can add to stereotypes [that they are "more valuable]."
→ [ ]는 접속사 that이 이끄는 명사절로, 앞의 명사 stereotypes와 동격 관계를 이룬다.

13행 It *feels strange* **to see** familiar things in new ways, … .
→ it이 가주어이고, to see 이하가 진주어이다.
→ feels strange는 「감각동사 + 형용사」 형태로, '이상하게 느껴지다'의 의미이다.

READING 2   The Coldest Desert

▶ **Reading Comprehension**
1 a   2 a   3 Very few plants live there   4 d

▶ **Grammar Inside Level 1**
Check Up 1 little   2 a few

　　사람들은 보통 사막을 많은 식물이나 동물이 없는 덥고 모래로 뒤덮인 곳으로 생각한다. 그리고 그곳에는 물이 많이 없기 때문에, 사람들은 그곳이 매우 건조하다고 믿는 경향이 있다.
　　지구의 많은 사막들이 이런 전형적인 설명에 들어맞는다. (A) 예를 들어, 아프리카의 사하라 사막은 지구상에서 가장 더운 곳 중 하나이다. (C) 그러나 모든 사막이 덥고 모래로 가득 찬 것은 아니다. (B) 사실, 세계에서 가장 큰 사막은 남극이다. 모래 대신에, 남극 대륙은 얼음으로 가득 차 있다. 그리고 그곳은 영하 89도까지 추워질 수 있다. 극소수의 식물들이 그곳에 살고 있어서, 먹이를 찾는 것은 어렵다. 이러한 이유로, 남극 대륙의 대부분 동물들은 육식이다.
　　사하라와 남극은 정말 다른 곳처럼 보인다. 하지만 둘 다 비나 습기가 거의 없다. 그래서 식물과 동물에게는

그곳에서 사는 것이 어렵다. 보다시피, 덥다는 것이 사막을 정의하지 않는다. 가장 큰 특징은 <u>건조하고 극단적인 온도를 가지는 것</u>이다.

어휘 desert 몡 사막   usually 뮈 보통, 대개   sandy 혱 모래로 뒤덮인   plant 몡 식물   tend to ~하는 경향이 있다
dry 혱 건조한   Earth 몡 지구   fit 동 들어맞다   typical 혱 전형적인   description 몡 설명, 기술, 서술
Antarctica 몡 남극 (대륙)   full of ~로 가득 찬   instead of ~ 대신에   for this reason 이러한 이유로   seem
like ~처럼 보이다, ~인 것 같다   moisture 몡 습기, 수분   define 동 정의하다   characteristic 몡 특징   [문제]
extreme 혱 극단적인   temperature 몡 온도, 기온

구문 2행 And **since** they don't have much water, people tend to believe they are very dry.
→ 접속사 since는 〈이유〉를 나타내며, '~하기 때문에'라는 의미이다.

4행 For example, the Sahara Desert in Africa is **one of the hottest places** on Earth.
→ 「one of the + 최상급 + 복수명사」는 '가장 ~한 …들 중 하나'라는 의미이다.

6행 But **not all** deserts are hot and full of sand.
→ every, all 등 〈전체〉를 나타내는 말과 〈부정〉을 나타내는 not이 함께 쓰이면 '모두 ~인 것은 아니다'라는 의미의 〈부분부정〉을 나타낸다.

8행 And it can get **as cold as** –89°C.
→ 「as + 형용사 + as」는 '~만큼 …한'의 의미이다.

12행 So **living there** is hard for plants and animals.
→ living there는 주어로 쓰인 동명사구이다.

13행 **As** you can see, *being hot* doesn't define a desert.
→ 접속사 as는 '~하듯이'라는 의미이다.
→ being hot은 주어로 쓰인 동명사구이다.

14행 The main characteristics are [being dry] **and** [having extreme temperatures].
→ 주격 보어 역할을 하는 동명사구 being dry와 having 이하가 접속사 and로 병렬 연결되었다.

● VOCABULARY INSIDE

Check Up 1 publish   2 bottom   3 description   4 characteristic   5 sandy   6 strange
7 define   8 focus

READING 1　The Coolest Music in the World

▶ **Reading Comprehension**
　1 a　2 b　3 c　4 melt a little each time they are played

▶ **Grammar Inside Starter**
　Check Up 1 그의 친구들을 만나기 위해　2 질문을 하기 위해

해석　　　　매년 겨울 스웨덴 북부에서는, 꽁꽁 언 이글루 모양의 연주회장 안에서 독특한 공연이 열린다. 사람들은 얼음 음악 오케스트라를 듣기 위해 따뜻한 옷을 입고 모인다. 연주회 동안, 각각의 음악가는 섬세한 주의를 요구하는 악기를 연주한다. 얼마나 연약하냐고? 그것은 손에서 녹을 수 있다! 놀랍게도, 악기들은 얼음으로 만들어진다.

　　　　얼음 음악 오케스트라는 바이올린, 기타, 드럼, 그리고 대형 실로폰을 포함하여 다양한 얼음 악기들을 연주한다. 현악기에 금속 현이 있긴 하지만, 주요 부분은 얼음으로 만들어진다. 중요한 건, 관악기가 없다는 것이다. 그것들이 음악가의 입김에 녹을 것이기 때문이다! 또한, 악기들은 소리를 유지하기 위해서 곡들 사이에 다시 조율되어야 한다. 그것들은 연주될 때마다 조금씩 녹기 때문이다.

　　　　공연 동안, 악기는 열이 없고, 색이 변하는 LED 조명으로 빛난다. 공연은 인상적이다. 하지만 아쉽게도, 그것은 관중이 너무 추워하거나 악기가 녹는 것을 막기 위해 짧게 유지되어야 한다!

어휘　**northern** 혱 북부의, 북쪽에 위치한　**unique** 혱 독특한　**performance** 몡 공연, 연주회　**take place** 개최되다, 일어나다　**frozen** 혱 꽁꽁 언 (**freeze** 동 얼(리)다; *얼 정도로 춥게 느끼다)　**igloo-shaped** 혱 이글루 모양의　**gather** 동 모이다　**delicate** 혱 섬세한 주의를 요구하는, 연약한　**instrument** 몡 기구; *악기　**melt** 동 녹다　**a variety of** 다양한, 여러 가지의　**including** 젠 ~을 포함하여　**xylophone** 몡 실로폰　**although** 젭 ~이긴 하지만　**stringed instrument** 현악기　**metal** 몡 금속　**string** 몡 줄; *(악기의) 현　**wind instrument** 관악기　**retune** 동 (악기를) 다시 조율하다　**maintain** 동 유지하다　**glow** 동 빛나다　**heatless** 혱 열이 없는　**impressive** 혱 인상적인, 인상 깊은　**prevent** 동 막다, 방지하다　**audience** 몡 청중, 관중　[문제] **appreciate** 동 감상하다　**breath** 몡 입김, 숨

구문　**5행** Surprisingly, the instruments **are made of** ice.
　　→ 「be + made of + 명사」는 '~로 만들어지다'라는 의미이다.

　　9행 Also, the instruments **must be retuned** between songs to maintain their sound.
　　→ must be retuned는 조동사(must)가 들어간 수동태로, '다시 조율되어야 한다'라는 의미이다.

　　11행 This is because they melt a little **each time** *they are* played.
　　→ 「each time + 주어 + 동사」는 '~가 …할 때마다'라는 의미이다.
　　→ each time이 이끄는 절에서 주어 they는 '연주되는' 대상인 the instruments를 가리키는 인칭대명사이므로, 「be + v-ed」 형태의 수동태(are played)가 쓰였다.

　　13행 But sadly, they must **be kept short** *to prevent* the audience **from freezing** and the instruments **from melting**!
　　→ be kept short는 '~을 …하게 유지하다'의 의미인 「keep + 목적어 + 형용사」를 수동태로 바꿔 쓴 형태이다.
　　→ to prevent 이하는 〈목적〉을 나타내는 부사적 용법의 to부정사구로, '~을 막기 위해'라는 의미이다.
　　→ 「prevent + 목적어 + from + v-ing」는 '~가 …하는 것을 막다'라는 의미이다.

▶ **Reading Comprehension**
  1 c   2 ice was rare   3 c   4 b

▶ **Grammar Inside Starter**
  Check Up 1 many places   2 any money

해석   요즘에, 얼음은 저렴하고 쉽게 구매될 수 있다. 하지만 냉장고가 발명되기 전에 얼음은 희귀했다. 이것은 보스턴 출신 남자인 Frederic Tudor가 19세기에 얼음 무역을 시작했을 때 바뀌었다. 그는 꽁꽁 언 겨울 연못에서 얼음을 가져다 세계의 더운 지역에 운송할 아이디어를 생각해냈다. 사람들은 이것이 불가능하다고 생각했다. "그것은 녹아버릴 거야!"라고 그들은 말했다.

처음에는, Tudor가 운송하려 했던 얼음의 대부분이 정말 녹아버렸다. 하지만 나중에, 그는 톱밥으로 얼음을 싸서 저장하는 방법을 알아냈다. 이는 그것이 더 천천히 녹게 했다. (고대에, 사람들이 얼음을 톱밥이나 소금 안에 보관했다.) 심지어 그가 180톤의 얼음을 인도의 캘커타로 운송했을 때도, 그것의 대부분은 녹지 않았다.

사업을 성장시키기 위해, Tudor는 자신의 상품을 훌륭하게 광고했다. 예를 들어, 그는 바텐더들에게 사용해 볼 무료 얼음을 제공했다. 그는 사람들이 그것을 좋아할 것을 알았다! 그의 사업은 1930년대에 전기 냉동고가 발명될 때까지 막대한 성공을 거두었다. Tudor의 창의력과 사업 기술은 그를 부유하게 만들었다!

어휘   cheap 혱 저렴한. 싼   easily 훈 쉽게   refrigerator 혱 냉장고   invent 동 발명하다   rare 혱 희귀한. 드문   begin 동 시작하다   trade 혱 무역, 교역   come up with ~을 생각해내다   frozen 혱 꽁꽁 언   pond 혱 연못   ship 혱 배, 선박; *동 *운송하다, 실어 나르다   part 혱 일부; *지역   impossible 혱 불가능한   melt 동 녹다   discover 동 발견하다; *알아내다   store 동 저장[보관]하다   pack 동 싸다, 포장하다   ancient 혱 고대의   salt 혱 소금   business 혱 사업   bartender 혱 바텐더   free 혱 자유로운; *무료의   huge 혱 막대한. 엄청난   success 혱 성공   electric 혱 전기의   freezer 혱 냉동고   creativity 혱 창의력. 창조성   skill 혱 기술   rich 혱 부유한   [문제] market 동 (상품을) 광고하다   brilliantly 훈 찬란하게; *훌륭하게   lower 동 낮추다

구문   1행 These days, ice is cheap and **can be bought** easily.
  → can be bought는 조동사(can)가 들어간 수동태로, '구매될 수 있다'의 의미이다.

  1행 But **before** refrigerators *were invented*, ice was rare.
  → before는 〈시간〉을 나타내는 접속사로, '~하기 전에'의 의미이다.
  → were invented는 「be + v-ed」 형태의 수동태이다.

  4행 He came up with the idea [to take ice from frozen winter ponds] **and** [ship ...].
  → 등위접속사 and로 to take ... ponds와 (to) ship 이하가 대등하게 연결되어 있다.

  9행 At first, most of the ice [Tudor tried to ship] *did melt*.
  → [ ]는 선행사 the ice를 수식하는 목적격 관계대명사절로, 앞에 that[which]이 생략되었다.
  → 동사를 강조하는 do[does/did]는 '정말[꼭] ~하다'의 의미로, 다음에 동사원형(melt)이 온다.

  10행 But later, he discovered a way to store the ice **by packing** it in sawdust.
  → 「by + v-ing」는 '~함으로써'라는 의미로, 〈수단〉 및 〈방법〉을 나타낸다.

  14행 For example, he **gave bartenders free ice *to try***.
  → 「give + 간접목적어 + 직접목적어」는 '~에게 …을 주다'의 의미이다.
  → to try는 '사용해 볼'의 의미로, 명사구 free ice를 수식하는 형용사적 용법의 to부정사이다.

UNIT 10 | Competition

pp. 61–66

READING 1   The World's First Spider

▶ **Reading Comprehension**
   1 d   2 d   3 a   4 smaller, legs, the first spider

▶ **Grammar Inside Starter**
   Check Up 1 to be   2 to stay

해석   아라크네는 젊은 그리스 여자였다. 그녀는 베를 짜는 데 매우 재능이 있었고 자랑하기 좋아했다. 직물의 여신인
아테나는 아라크네의 허풍에 대해 들었다. 그녀는 자기 자신을 늙은 여자로 변장해서 아라크네와 이야기하기로
결심했다. "어디서 베를 짜는 법을 배웠나요?"라고 그녀가 물었다. "이 재능은 아테나가 당신에게 준 것인가요?" 그러나
아라크네는 "물론 아니에요. 저는 스스로 터득했어요!"라고 대답했다.

이것이 아테나를 화나게 해서, 그녀 자신을 직물의 여신의 모습으로 드러냈다. "나한테 도전하겠느냐?"라고 그녀가
소리쳤다. "그러면 시작하지!" 아라크네와 아테나는 재빨리 베를 짜기 시작했다. 아테나는 신들의 놀라운 이미지를
만들었다. 그녀의 묘사에서, 그들은 영웅적으로 보였고 선행을 베풀었다. 아라크네 또한 신들의 놀라운 이미지들을
만들었다. 하지만 그녀의 묘사에서, 그들은 화가 나 있었고 어리석었다.

아라크네의 묘사는 아테나를 격노하게 했다. "어떻게 네가 감히!"라고 그녀가 소리쳤다. "너는 벌을 받아야겠다."
아테나는 막대기를 잡고 아라크네를 쳤다. 신기하게도, 아라크네는 더 작아졌고, 다리들이 자라, 최초의 거미가 되었다!
"이제 너는 온종일 베를 짤 수 있겠구나."라고 아테나가 말했다.

어휘   spider 명 거미   talented 형 재능이 있는 (talent 명 재능)   weave 동 (베 등을) 짜다, 엮다   brag 동 자랑하다,
떠벌리다   goddess 명 여신 (god 명 신)   boast 명 허풍, 자랑   disguise 동 변장하다   reply 동 대답하다
reveal 동 드러내다, 밝히다   challenge 동 도전하다   yell 동 소리치다   picture 명 사진; *묘사   heroic 형
영웅적인, 용감무쌍한   perform 동 (수)행하다   deed 명 행동   foolish 형 어리석은   furious 형 격노한, 몹시 화가 난
scream 동 소리치다   punish 동 (처)벌하다   grab 동 (붙)잡다, 움켜잡다   stick 명 막대기   magically 부 신기하게도

구문   1행 She [**was** very **talented at weaving**] *and* [loved to brag].
   → be talented at은 '~에 재능이 있다'의 의미로, 동명사 weaving이 전치사의 at의 목적어로 쓰였다.
   → 등위접속사 and로 was ... weaving과 loved to brag가 대등하게 연결되어 있다.

   3행 She decided to **disguise** *herself* **as** an old woman and talk to Arachne.
   → disguise A as B는 'A를 B로 변장하다'의 의미이다.
   → to부정사 to disguise의 목적어로 Athena 자기 자신을 지칭하는 재귀대명사 herself가 쓰였다.

5행 "**Was** this talent **given** to you by Athena?"
→ 「be + 주어 + v-ed ...?」 형태의 수동태 의문문이다.

7행 This **made Athena angry**, so she *revealed* **herself** *as* the goddess of weaving.
→ 「make + 목적어 + 형용사」는 '~가 ⋯하게 하다'의 의미이다. 동사 make의 목적격 보어로 형용사 angry가 쓰였다.
→ reveal A as B는 'A를 B로 드러내다[밝히다]'의 의미이다.
→ 동사 revealed의 목적어로 Athena 자기 자신을 지칭하는 재귀대명사 herself가 쓰였다.

8행 "You **wish to challenge** me?" she yelled.
→ 동사 wish는 to부정사(to challenge)를 목적어로 취한다.

9행 Arachne and Athena quickly **started to weave**.
→ 동사 start는 목적어로 to부정사(to weave)와 동명사(weaving) 모두 취할 수 있다.

14행 "You **must be punished**."
→ must be punished는 조동사 must를 포함한 수동태로, '벌을 받아야 한다'의 의미이다.

READING 2   The Rower and the Ducks

▶ **Reading Comprehension**
1 b   2 d   3 d   4 c

▶ **Grammar Inside Level 1**
Check Up 1 running   2 uploading

해석   모든 사람들은 이기는 것을 좋아한다. 하지만 어떤 사람들은 삶에 있어서 승리보다 더 중요한 것이 있다는 것을 안다.

Bobby Pearce는 이런 사람들 중 한 명이었다. 그는 호주 출신의 뛰어난 조정 선수였다. 1928년 올림픽에서, 그는 1인 조정 경기 종목에 출전 중이었다. 이런 유형의 경주에서, 각 보트에는 두 개의 노를 가진 한 명의 선수가 있다. 경기의 중반에, Pearce는 쉽게 이기고 있었다. 그런데 그때 그는 예상치 못한 무언가를 보았다. 한 오리 가족이 그의 보트 바로 앞을 가로질러 가고 있었다!

Pearce는 오리들을 다치게 하고 싶지 않아서, 노를 젓는 것을 멈추었다. 하지만 그의 상대편은 계속 노를 저었고 선두에 섰다. 오리들이 지나간 뒤에, Pearce는 다시 노를 젓기 시작했다. 놀랍게도, 그는 상대편을 따라잡았고 경주에서 승리했다!

결국, Pearce는 금메달을 땄고 그 종목에서 세계 기록을 세웠다. 하지만 그는 오리 가족의 생명을 보호하기 위해 경주에서 패배할 위험을 무릅썼다!

어휘   rower ⓟ 노 젓는 사람 (row ⓥ 노를 젓다)   duck ⓟ 오리   win ⓥ 이기다; (메달 등을) 획득하다   compete ⓥ 경쟁하다; *(시합 등에) 출전[참가]하다   single ⓐ 1인용의; (단) 하나의   event ⓟ 사건, 일; *종목, 경기   race ⓟ 경주   each ⓐ 각각의   halfway ⓟ 중반부에   cross ⓥ 가로지르다, 건너다   directly ⓟ 바로   in front of ~ 앞에   opponent ⓟ (대회 등의) 상대   take the lead 선두에 서다   pass ⓥ 지나가다   amazingly ⓟ 놀랍게도   catch up with ~을 따라잡다   eventually ⓟ 결국, 끝내   set a record 기록을 세우다   risk ⓥ ~의 위험을 무릅쓰다   lose ⓥ 잃어버리다; *패배하다   protect ⓥ 보호하다, 지키다   [문제] solution ⓟ 해결(책)   meaning ⓟ 의미   beat ⓥ 패배시키다, 이기다   unexpected ⓐ 예기치 않은, 예상 밖의   hurt ⓥ 다치게 하다

1행 ... understand [that there are *more important* things in life *than* winning].

→ [ ]는 동사 understand의 목적어 역할을 하는 명사절이다.

→ 「형용사 비교급 + than」은 '~보다 더 …한'의 의미이다.

4행 ..., he **was competing** in the single sculls event.

→ 「was/were + v-ing」는 과거 진행형으로 '~하고 있었다'라는 의미이다.

9행 After the ducks **had passed**, Pearce *began rowing* again.

→ had passed는 과거보다 더 이전의 일을 나타내는 「had + v-ed」 형태의 과거완료 시제이다. 오리들이 지나간 것이 주절의 동사 began보다 더 이전의 일임을 나타낸다.

→ 동사 begin은 목적어로 동명사(rowing)와 to부정사(to row)를 모두 취할 수 있다.

13행 But he **risked losing** the race *to protect* the lives of a family of ducks!

→ 동사 risk는 동명사(losing)를 목적어로 취하며, 「risk + v-ing」는 '~할 위험을 무릅쓰다'라는 의미이다.

→ to protect 이하는 '~을 보호하기 위해'라는 뜻으로, 〈목적〉을 나타내는 부사적 용법의 to부정사구이다.

● **VOCABULARY INSIDE**

Check Up **1** reveal **2** furious **3** event **4** compete **5** risk **6** protect
7 deed **8** talented

UNIT 11 | Sea

pp. 67–72

READING 1 | Ribbon Eels

▶ **Reading Comprehension**
1 b **2** (1) T (2) F (3) T **3** (1) male (2) (bright) blue (3) yellow **4** c

▶ **Grammar Inside Starter**
Check Up before

해석

리본 장어는 놀라운 외형을 가진 해양 생물이다. 길고 납작한 몸이 있어, 이것은 꼭 물속에서 흔들리는 화려한 리본처럼 보인다. 이 아름다운 장어는 약 1미터까지 자랄 수 있고 20년까지 살 수 있다.

리본 장어는 자라면서, 색이 변한다. 어릴 때, 그것은 등에 얇은 노란색의 지느러미가 달린 검은색 몸통을 가진다. 점점 더 커지면서, 그것의 몸통은 밝은 파란색으로 바뀌고, 마침내 모두 노란색으로 바뀐다.

놀랍게도, 나이가 들면 장어의 성별도 바뀐다. 모든 리본 장어는 검은색 몸을 가진 수컷으로 태어난다. 리본 장어가 파란색으로 바뀌면, 그것은 완전히 다 자란 수컷이 된 것이다. 노란색으로 바뀌면, 그것은 암컷이 되고 알을 낳을 수 있다! 안타깝게도, 그것은 알을 낳은 뒤 약 한 달 이내에 죽는다. 그래서, 야생에서 노란색 리본 장어를 발견하는 것은 쉽지 않다.

어휘 eel 영 장어   creature 영 생물, 생명체   amazing 형 놀라운   appearance 영 외형, 모습   flat 형 납작한, 평평한   wave 동 흔들리다   grow 동 자라다, 크다   up to ~까지   thin 형 얇은, 가는   back 영 등   turn 동 돌다; *(~한 상태로) 변하다, ~이 되다   bright 형 (색 등이) 밝은   surprisingly 부 놀랍게도   gender 영 성별   be born 태어나다   male 영 수컷   fully 부 완전히, 충분히   adult 형 다 자란, 성인의   female 영 암컷   lay 동 놓다, 두다; *(알을) 낳다   unfortunately 부 안타깝게도, 불행히도   within 전 ~ 이내에[안에]   wild 영 야생, 자연   [문제] predator 영 포식자   aquarium 영 수족관   surroundings 영 주변 환경

구문

1행 ..., it **looks** just **like** a colorful ribbon [waving in the water].
→ 「look like + 명사」는 '~처럼 보이다'의 의미이다.
→ [ ]는 명사구 a colorful ribbon을 수식하는 현재분사구이다.

3행 This beautiful eel can grow [to be about one meter long] ... .
→ [ ]는 '(~해서) …가 되다'라는 의미의 〈결과〉를 나타내는 부사적 용법의 to부정사구이다.

5행 **As** a ribbon eel grows, its color changes.
→ as는 '~하면서, ~함에 따라'라는 의미의 접속사로 쓰였다.

6행 As it **gets bigger**, its body *turns bright blue* and, ...
→ 「get + 형용사 비교급」은 '점점 더 ~해지다'의 의미이다.
→ 「turn + 형용사」는 '~로 변하다'의 의미이다. 동사 turns의 주격 보어로 형용사구 bright blue가 쓰였다.

9행 When a ribbon eel turns blue, it **has become** a fully adult male.
→ 「have/has + v-ed」는 현재완료 시제로, 이 문장에서는 〈완료〉의 의미를 나타낸다.

12행 So, **it** is not easy **to find** yellow ribbon eels in the wild.
→ it은 가주어이고 to find 이하의 to부정사구가 진주어이다.

READING 2   Magellan's Great Discovery

▶ **Reading Comprehension**
1 b   2 d   3 (1) T (2) F   4 a

▶ **Grammar Inside Starter**
Check Up but

해석   태평양은 지구의 오대양 중 가장 깊고 크다. 그 이름 자체는 16세기에 포르투갈 항해사 Ferdinand Magellan이 지었다. 그와 그의 선원들은 1519년 인도네시아의 향료 제도로 가는 항로를 찾기 위해 스페인에서 출항했다. 그 당시에, 이 섬들은 세계에서 가장 많은 후추, 육두구, 그리고 정향을 생산했다.

항해하는 동안, 그의 작은 무리의 배들은 낯선 바다를 우연히 발견했다. 그곳의 고요함 때문에, 그는 그 바다를 Mar Pacífico라고 불렀다. 이것은 '평화로운 바다'를 의미했고, '태평양'이라는 이름은 여기에서 유래되었다. 그는 향료 제도가 매우 가까이에 있다고 믿었지만, 그것은 사실이 아닌 것으로 판명 났다. 안타깝게도, Magellan 자신과 그의 선원들 대부분은 바다에서 죽었다.

그 이름에도 불구하고, 태평양은 매우 활발한 수역이다. 셀 수 없이 많은 독특한 생물들이 그것의 아주 깊은 곳에 살고 있다. 오늘날까지, 우리는 여전히 이 거대한 바다를 많이 탐험하지 못했다.

어휘   discovery 영 발견   the Pacific Ocean 태평양   deep 형 깊은 (depth 영 깊이)   major 형 주요한   ocean

명 대양, 바다   navigator 명 항해사, 조종사   crew 명 선원   route 명 항로, 경로   produce 동 생산하다   pepper 명 후추   voyage 명 항해, 여행   come upon ~을 우연히 발견하다[만나다]   unfamiliar 형 낯선, 익숙하지 않은   calmness 명 고요(함), 평온(함)   peaceful 형 평화로운   derived from ~에서 유래된[파생된]   prove 동 판명되다, 드러나다   untrue 형 사실이 아닌, 허위의   active 형 활발한, 왕성한   body of water 수역   countless 형 셀 수 없이 많은   unique 형 독특한   beneath 전 ~ 밑[아래]에   explore 동 탐험하다   enormous 형 거대한   [문제] due to ~ 때문에   despite 전 ~에도 불구하고   against 전 ~에 대항하여

구문

1행 The Pacific Ocean is **the deepest** and **largest** of the five major oceans on Earth.
→ deepest와 largest는 각각 형용사 deep과 large의 최상급이며, 최상급 앞에는 보통 the를 붙인다.

3행 The name **itself** *was given* by Portuguese navigator Ferdinand Magellan ... .
→ itself는 명사 the name을 강조하는 재귀대명사로, '그 자체'라는 의미이다.
→ was given은 「be + v-ed」 형태의 수동태이다.

5행 He and his crew sailed from Spain in 1519 **to find** a route ... .
→ to find 이하는 '~을 찾기 위해'라는 뜻으로, 〈목적〉을 나타내는 부사적 용법의 to부정사구이다.

13행 He believed [the Spice Islands were very near], but that would *prove untrue*.
→ [ ]는 동사 believed의 목적어 역할을 하는 명사절로, 앞에 접속사 that이 생략되어 있다.
→ 「prove + 형용사」는 '~로 판명 나다'의 의미이다. 동사 would prove의 주격 보어로 형용사 untrue가 쓰였다.

17행 To this day, we still **haven't explored** much of this enormous ocean.
→ 「have/has + v-ed」는 현재완료 시제로, 이 문장에서는 〈완료〉의 의미를 나타낸다.

● **VOCABULARY INSIDE**

Check Up 1 flat 2 route 3 amazing 4 peaceful 5 major 6 discovery
7 appearance 8 wild

UNIT 12 | Environment

READING 1   Two out of a Thousand

▶ **Reading Comprehension**
1 b 2 c 3 c 4 two, humans

▶ **Grammar Inside Level 1**
Check Up 1 if 2 because

해석   바다거북은 오래 산다. 하지만 그들의 삶은 쉽지 않다. (C) 암컷 거북이는 해변에 알을 낳는다. (A) 그러나 매 1,000개의 알 중 800개만이 부화한다. (B) 비록 새끼는 겨우 당신의 손 만한 크기이지만, 그들은 바다를 향해 나아가야

한다. 그들은 다른 동물들에 의해 공격받고, 그들의 절반은 잡아먹힌다. 바다에 도달한 후에, 마지막 남은 400마리의 거북이들은 상어와 돌고래 같은 새로운 포식 동물들을 피해야 하므로 여전히 위험에 처해 있다. 겨우 50퍼센트만이 최대 크기까지 자라게 된다. 보통, 다 자란 이 거북이들 중 20마리 정도가 살아남아 알을 낳기 위해 해변으로 돌아간다.

　　하지만 요즘, 바다거북은 더 큰 위험에 직면하는데, 바로 인간이다. 고기잡이 그물과 오염이 살아남은 다 자란 바다거북의 수를 고작 두 마리로 줄여 버린다. 다시 말해서, 800마리의 새끼 바다거북이들이 해변에서 부화하면, 오직 0.25퍼센트만이 부모가 되는 것이다.

　　바다거북에게 생존은 항상 어려웠다. 하지만 인간이 그 문제를 훨씬 더 악화시키고 있다.

어휘　out of ~의 밖으로; *~ 중에　sea turtle 바다거북　hatch ⑧ 부화하다　make one's way to ~로 나아가다 ocean ⑱ 바다, 대양　female ⑲ 암컷의　lay ⑧ (알을) 낳다　beach ⑱ 해변, 바닷가　attack ⑧ 공격하다　half ⑲ (절)반　reach ⑧ 도달하다　last ⑲ 마지막의; *마지막 남은　in danger 위험에 처한 (danger ⑱ 위험)　avoid ⑧ 피하다　predator ⑱ 포식 동물, 포식자　such as ~와 같은　shark ⑱ 상어　dolphin ⑱ 돌고래　full ⑲ 가득한; *최대[최고]의　normally ⑨ 보통　adult ⑱ 성체; *다 자란　survive ⑧ 살아남다, 생존하다 (survival ⑱ 생존) return ⑧ 돌아가다　breed ⑧ (알·새끼를) 낳다　face ⑧ 직면하다　human ⑱ 인간, 인류　fishing net 고기잡이 그물, 어망　pollution ⑱ 오염, 공해　reduce ⑧ 줄이다, 낮추다　[문제] mysterious ⑲ 불가사의한

구문

　4행 They **are attacked by** other animals, and *half of them* **are** eaten.
　→ are attacked by와 are eaten은 「be + v-ed(+ by)」 형태의 수동태이다.
　→ 「half of + (대)명사」는 (대)명사(them)에 수를 일치시키므로, be동사로 are가 쓰였다.

　5행 **After** they reach the water, the last 400 turtles are still in danger … .
　→ 접속사 after는 '~한 후에[뒤에]'라는 의미이다.

　7행 Normally, about 20 of these adults survive and return to the beach **to breed**.
　→ to breed는 '알을 낳기 위해'라는 의미로, 〈목적〉을 나타내는 부사적 용법의 to부정사이다.

　10행 … pollution reduce **the number of** surviving adult sea turtles to just two.
　→ the number of는 '~의 수'라는 의미이다.

　11행 …, only 0.25% will become parents **themselves**.
　→ 재귀대명사 themselves는 명사 parents를 강조하며, 생략 가능하다.

　13행 Survival **has** always **been** difficult for sea turtles.
　→ 「have/has + v-ed」는 현재완료 시제로, 이 문장에서는 〈계속〉을 나타낸다.

　14행 But humans are **making the problem** *much worse*.
　→ 「make + 목적어 + 형용사」는 '~을 …하게 만들다'라는 뜻이다. 동사 are making의 목적격 보어로 형용사구 much worse가 쓰였다.
　→ 부사 much는 '훨씬'이란 의미로, 비교급 worse를 강조한다.

READING 2　The Art of Erasing

▶ **Reading Comprehension**
1 d　2 dirty, brushes　3 reverse graffiti　4 d

▶ **Grammar Inside Level 1**
Check Up　1 목적어　2 보어

대부분의 사람들은 그래피티가 벽이나 표면에 페인트를 더한 것의 결과라고 생각한다. 하지만 무언가를 지움으로써 그래피티를 만들어 내는 것도 가능하다는 것을 알고 있었는가? 이런 예술 유형은 리버스 그래피티라고 불린다.

리버스 그래피티는, 깨끗한 그래피티라고도 알려져 있으며, 문자 그대로 전통적인 그래피티에 대한 발상을 뒤집는다. 우선, 리버스 그래피티 예술가들은 더러운 표면을 찾는다. 그다음 그들은 붓과 물 호스로 때의 일부분을 깨끗이 닦아낸다. 이미지는 깨끗한 부분과 더러운 부분 간의 대조에 의해 만들어진다. 리버스 그래피티는 더러운 도로 표지판과 더러운 터널 벽에서 발견되어왔는데, 이 새로운 추세는 전 세계에 걸쳐 확산되고 있다.

최근에, 리버스 그래피티는 광고의 한 유형으로 사용되고 있다. 포스터와 전단 같은 광고는 많은 재료를 사용하고 쓰레기를 만든다. 하지만, 리버스 그래피티는 오로지 붓, 물, 그리고 창의력만을 필요로 한다! 또한, 그것은 일시적이고 해로운 페인트를 사용하지 않는다. 다시 말해서, 이것은 아주 환경친화적이다!

erase 통 지우다　**graffiti** 명 낙서; *그래피티　**result** 명 결과, 결실　**add** 통 더하다, 덧붙이다　**wall** 명 벽　**surface** 명 표면, 지면　**possible** 형 가능한　**create** 통 만들다, 창조하다 (**creativity** 명 창의력)　**known as** ~로 알려진　**literally** 부 문자 그대로　**reverse** 형 반대의, 거꾸로 된; 통 뒤집다, 뒤바꾸다　**traditional** 형 전통적인　**dirty** 형 더러운 (**dirt** 명 때, 더러운 것)　**clean away** 깨끗이 치우다　**contrast** 명 대조, 차이　**road sign** 도로 표지판　**trend** 명 추세, 동향　**spread** 통 펼치다; *확산되다, 퍼지다　**recently** 부 최근에　**form** 명 유형, 종류　**advertising** 명 광고 (사업) (**advertisement** 명 광고)　**leaflet** 명 (광고나 선전용) 전단　**material** 명 직물, 천; *재료　**waste** 명 낭비; *쓰레기, 폐기물　**require** 통 필요하다, 요구하다　**temporary** 형 일시적인, 임시의　**harmful** 형 해로운, 유해한　**environmentally friendly** 환경친화적인

2행 But did you know [that *it*'s also possible *to create* graffiti **by erasing** something]?
→ [ ]는 동사 know의 목적어 역할을 하는 명사절이다.
→ 접속사 that이 이끄는 명사절에서 it은 가주어이고 to create 이하의 to부정사구가 진주어이다.
→ 「by + v-ing」는 '~하면서, ~함으로써'라는 의미로, 〈수단〉 및 〈방법〉을 나타낸다.

5행 Reverse graffiti, **also known as clean graffiti**, literally reverses the idea ... .
→ also known as clean graffiti는 Reverse graffiti를 부연 설명하는 삽입구이다.

8행 Images **are made by** the contrast *between* the clean part *and* the dirty part.
→ are made by는 「be + v-ed + by」 형태의 수동태로, '~에 의해 만들어지다'라는 의미이다.
→ between A and B는 'A와 B 간[사이]의'라는 의미이다.

9행 Reverse graffiti **has been seen** on dirty road signs ..., and this new trend *is spreading* ... .
→ has been seen은 「have/has + been + v-ed」 형태의 현재완료 수동태이다. 이 문장에서 현재완료는 〈계속〉을 의미한다.
→ is spreading은 「be + v-ing」 형태의 현재진행형으로 '확산되고 있다'의 의미이다.

● VOCABULARY INSIDE

Check Up　**1** attacked　**2** harmful　**3** hatch　**4** form　**5** laying　**6** reduce
7 reverse　**8** Temporary

READING
Inside
Workbook

STARTER

UNIT 01 | Origins
pp. 2–5

VOCABULARY TEST 1

01 전통 02 노예; 노예 제도 03 해상 운송
04 비슷한, 유사한 05 심장 박동 06 오늘날에는
07 놀라운, 굉장한 08 어조, 말투; 음색, 음조
09 현대의, 근대의 10 막대기 11 시작되다, 시작하다
12 특허받다 13 공연 14 (소리가) 큰, 시끄러운
15 인상적인, 감명 깊은 16 기구, 악기 17 펼치다;
퍼지다, 확산되다 18 만들어 내다 19 영감을 주다
20 또렷하게, 분명히 21 결국 22 (속이) 빈
23 부유한; 풍부한 24 consult 25 miss
26 coastal 27 capture 28 heart
29 acoustic 30 birth 31 tiny 32 noise
33 chest 34 scrape 35 metal 36 산책하러
가다 37 둘둘 말다 38 무료로 39 많은 40 다양한

VOCABULARY TEST 2

A ⓑ B ⓑ C 1 instrument 2 impressive
3 noise 4 hollow D 1 go for a walk
2 a range of 3 rolled up

GRAMMAR TEST

A 1 met 2 make 3 wrote 4 play
B 1 broke 2 read 3 bought 4 drank
C 1 Did you enjoy
  2 He didn't play
  3 My dad didn't clean
  4 Did they go

WRITING TEST

A 1 They didn't have drums
  2 is used in many kinds
  3 named René Laennec went for
  4 making the tiny noise very loud
  5 were captured and brought
B 1 to make a tube
  2 inspired by this idea
  3 them from drumming
  4 saw two boys playing
  5 decided to play the crates

UNIT 02 | Economics
pp. 6–9

VOCABULARY TEST 1

01 달리다; 운영하다 02 모든; 매 ~, ~마다 03 (일의
대가 등을) 지불하다 04 고르다, 선택하다 05 상품,
제품 06 고용하다 07 정확히 08 가정의
09 낮은 10 사실 11 가격 12 사업 13 격려하다;
권하다, 장려하다 14 세계적인 15 약, 약물
16 종업원, 직원 17 상상하다 18 야망, 포부
19 소비자 20 매우 큰, 거대한 21 흔히, 보통
22 방법 23 고객, 손님 24 worldwide 25 fool
26 present 27 public 28 decision
29 expensive 30 servant 31 spread
32 cost 33 right 34 cheap 35 innovative
36 ~을 대신하여 37 ~을 내놓다[제안하다] 38 감기에
걸리다 39 ~ 밖으로; ~ 중에(서) 40 ~에 영향을
미치다

VOCABULARY TEST 2

A ⓒ B ⓒ C 1 encourage 2 right
3 decision 4 hire D 1 have an effect on
2 came up with 3 on your behalf

GRAMMAR TEST

A 1 strange 2 sad 3 beautiful
  4 me a bookworm
B 1 heavy 2 sweet 3 happy
  4 his room clean 5 her a famous actress
C 1 이 꽃들은 좋은 냄새가 난다.
  2 이 스웨터는 부드럽게 느껴진다.
  3 그 영화는 나를 슬프게 했다.
  4 그 머그잔은 차를 따뜻하게 유지했다.

WRITING TEST

A 1 You want to buy
  2 This made Martha's salon
  3 might sound too expensive
  4 to save money for
  5 facts about their products sound
B 1 sounds much cheaper
  2 didn't want to hire
  3 encouraged Martha to open
  4 the right to use
  5 Instead of being paid

UNIT 03 | Jobs
pp. 10–13

VOCABULARY TEST 1

01 의무; 임무, 직무   02 능숙하게, 솜씨 있게   03 항공기
04 완료하다, 끝마치다   05 기술자   06 비행기
07 준비된   08 여행, 이동   09 제거하다   10 거리
11 뿌리다   12 연락   13 조명   14 시원한; 차갑게 하다
15 다루다, 처리하다   16 두꺼운   17 혼자   18 온도
19 조심히   20 얇은   21 습도   22 할 수 있게 하다
23 먼지   24 athlete   25 layer   26 conditions
27 safely   28 pilot   29 unexpected   30 affect
31 complicated   32 perform   33 flight
34 emergency   35 land   36 이륙하다
37 서로   38 수천의; 수많은   39 한 번에   40 ~을
관리하다[돌보다]

VOCABULARY TEST 2

A ⓓ   B ⓑ   C 1 unexpected   2 hurt
3 remove   4 complicated
D 1 take off   2 at a time   3 Thousands of

GRAMMAR TEST

A 1 asked   2 to clean   3 showed
　 4 to come   5 to save   6 to finish
B 1 sent him the files
　 2 gave me some advice
　 3 told me to drink
　 4 advised her to accept
　 5 asked her to join
　 6 lent me some books
　 7 made me a new chair

WRITING TEST

A 1 be thicker and less cold
　 2 hurt themselves from jumping
　 3 give the pilot information
　 4 might help one aircraft land
　 5 make sure that the planes
B 1 is responsible for
　 2 enables athletes to perform
　 3 allow skaters to perform
　 4 are needed to make
　 5 It's important to adjust

UNIT 04 | Technology
pp. 14–17

VOCABULARY TEST 1

01 결과   02 센서, 감지기   03 만들다, 창조하다
04 거리   05 (쓰레기)통   06 결정, 판단
07 친환경적인   08 동네, 이웃   09 신호   10 모퉁이
11 여러, 몇몇의   12 완전히, 전적으로   13 최첨단의
14 기구   15 위험한   16 경고하다   17 자유로운;
무료의   18 구역, 장소   19 예보, 예측   20 이미,
벌써   21 예상하다   22 자료, 데이터   23 정보
24 previous   25 weather   26 access
27 compare   28 place   29 highly   30 grab
31 crush   32 accurate   33 advanced
34 collection   35 process   36 ~을 들여다보다
37 ~할 형편이 되다   38 (소리·빛·냄새 등)을 내다
[발하다]   39 ~을 입다[신다]   40 수많은

VOCABULARY TEST 2

A ⓒ   B ⓓ   C 1 dangerous   2 free
3 previous   4 bin   D 1 afford to   2 see into
3 gives out

GRAMMAR TEST

A 1 can't   2 Can   3 must   4 have to
B 1 지불할 필요가 없다   2 주차해서는 안 된다
　 3 쓸 수 없다
C 1 don't have to wait for her
　 2 must[have to] follow the school rules
　 3 can speak four languages
　 4 must[have to] carry your passport

WRITING TEST

A 1 Something new is coming
　 2 makes a neighborhood better
　 3 give us predictions
　 4 have to use tons of
　 5 that each smart bin is
B 1 going to rain
　 2 enjoy using the internet
　 3 are created by people
　 4 cannot[can't] afford to pay
　 5 can compare the results with

UNIT 05 | Solutions pp. 18–21

VOCABULARY TEST 1

01 직물, 천; 재료   02 쓰레기   03 수도   04 특이한, 흔치 않은   05 지역[현지]의   06 광고   07 흡수하다, 빨아들이다   08 (물에) 뜨다   09 오염 (물질)
10 모으다   11 저장[보관]하다   12 보여 주다, 나타내다
13 증가하다, 늘다   14 만들다   15 정화하다
16 제거하다   17 항구   18 빨아들이다, 흡수하다
19 수도꼭지   20 무기   21 무거운; 극심한
22 제공[공급]하다   23 ~ 아래에   24 attach
25 desert   26 traffic   27 billboard   28 natural
29 run   30 release   31 filter   32 thirsty
33 effective   34 atmosphere   35 purify
36 ~로 만들어진   37 ~을 흡수하다   38 ~ 때문에
39 자력으로, 도움을 받지 않고   40 설치하다

VOCABULARY TEST 2

A ⓐ   B ⓐ   C 1 weapon   2 desert   3 store
4 float   D 1 by himself   2 due to   3 set up

GRAMMAR TEST

A 1 Watching   2 playing   3 meeting
　4 passing
B 1 am eating   2 is getting   3 are running
C 1 teaching Spanish
　2 He is walking
　3 She is dancing
　4 Drinking too much soda

WRITING TEST

A 1 is located in a desert
　2 more than 90 liters of water
　3 It was invented by
　4 made of natural materials
　5 to fight these problems
B 1 floating garbage bin
　2 is increasing
　3 Using the Seabin
　4 are still used as
　5 to remove oil from

UNIT 06 | Cooperation pp. 22–25

VOCABULARY TEST 1

01 식이, 식단   02 바로, 정확히   03 남은   04 추가의
05 참여[참가]하다   06 일어나다, 발생하다   07 연기
08 (사업) 파트너, 동업자   09 제대로 된, 적절한
10 슬로건, 표어   11 인근의, 가까운 곳의
12 선택하다, 고르다   13 예(시)   14 경우
15 제안하다; 암시[시사]하다   16 식사, 끼니   17 자선 (단체)   18 인간   19 품목, 항목   20 졸업자
21 설립하다, 세우다   22 꿀   23 간단한, 단순한
24 join   25 donate   26 cost   27 convenient
28 benefit   29 relationship   30 return
31 calm   32 follow   33 cooperate   34 guide
35 organization   36 grow   37 call
38 ~ 덕분에   39 ~을 부르다   40 어려움에 처한

VOCABULARY TEST 2

A ⓐ   B ⓑ   C 1 meals   2 guide
3 relationship   4 choose   D 1 in need
2 call out   3 Thanks to

GRAMMAR TEST

A 1 big   2 as   3 ones   4 it
B 1 one   2 They   3 ones   4 it
C 1 as old as Amy
　2 as hot as that tea
　3 as tall as that oak tree
　4 as fast as that car

WRITING TEST

A 1 ones that are hard
　2 as simple as eating
　3 used to give a meal
　4 who cooperate with honeyguides
　5 named Mealshare lets you
B 1 The number keeps growing
　2 Birds called honeyguides
　3 Mealshare was founded
　4 having a special relationship
　5 Helping someone in need

UNIT 07 | Sports pp. 26–29

VOCABULARY TEST 1

01 모양, 형태   02 (손 등으로) 대다, 만지다   03 장소;
놓다, 두다   04 (대회·논쟁 등의) 상대   05 잔디(밭)
06 잃다   07 인기   08 중앙, 한가운데   09 밀다
10 금속   11 영향; 효과   12 (차츰) 쌓다[늘리다]
13 단순한, 간단한   14 대리자, 대용품; 교체 선수
15 신호   16 대신에   17 규칙, 원칙   18 원래의,
본래의   19 나무로 된   20 사진, 그림; 상상하다
21 반응하다   22 인기   23 물속에서; 물속의, 수중의
24 half   25 ring   26 score   27 participant
28 during   29 cause   30 travel
31 professional   32 soft   33 above
34 bounce   35 hard   36 goal   37 숨을 참다
38 훈련을 치다   39 ~로 만들어진[구성된]   40 튀어
오르다; (원래의 모양으로) 되돌아가다

VOCABULARY TEST 2

A ⓑ   B ⓒ   C 1 half   2 react   3 signal
4 opponent   D 1 made of   2 hold your
breath   3 hit a home run

GRAMMAR TEST

A 1 bigger   2 better   3 heavier
  4 more interesting
B 1 than   2 than   3 more difficult   4 harder
C 1 higher than   2 faster than
  3 worse than   4 wiser than

WRITING TEST

A 1 makes the ball go farther
  2 like bouncing a ball
  3 is placed in the middle
  4 will travel more than
  5 Next time you want to
B 1 are shorter than
  2 it is safer than
  3 If he uses
  4 causes the ball to lose
  5 surprised to hear that

UNIT 08 | Geography pp. 30–33

VOCABULARY TEST 1

01 맨 위, 윗면   02 건조한   03 지구   04 목적, 목표
05 또 다른   06 낯선   07 보통, 대개   08 아래에,
밑에   09 익숙한, 친숙한   10 실제로, 정말로
11 극단적인   12 관점, 시각   13 발행[출판]하다
14 부유한   15 모래로 뒤덮인   16 국가, 나라
17 사막   18 정의하다   19 실수, 잘못   20 지도
21 가치 있는   22 식물   23 지역, 구역   24 typical
25 description   26 temperature
27 stereotype   28 importance   29 differently
30 moisture   31 fit   32 bottom
33 characteristic   34 Antarctica   35 focus
36 ~로 가득 찬   37 ~에 싫증이 난   38 ~에서 나오다
[생산되다]   39 ~ 대신에   40 ~을 가중하다, ~에
더하다

VOCABULARY TEST 2

A ⓐ   B ⓓ   C 1 mistake   2 publish
3 extreme   4 define   D 1 tired of   2 full
of   3 Instead of

GRAMMAR TEST

A 1 a few   2 little   3 a little   4 few
B 1 a few coins   2 to meet the singer   3 a few
hours   4 It, to wake up   5 a little space
C 1 It is important to know yourself.
  2 It is natural to feel sleepy at night
  3 It is hard to speak English fluently.

WRITING TEST

A 1 as cold as −89℃
  2 gave the world a new perspective
  3 Not all deserts are
  4 stereotypes that they are
  5 to make people think
  6 Since they don't have much water
B 1 Being hot doesn't define
  2 Living there is
  3 one of the hottest places
  4 It feels strange to see

UNIT 09 | Ice pp. 34–37

VOCABULARY TEST 1

01 유지하다　02 기구; 악기　03 열이 없는　04 꽁꽁 언
05 희귀한, 드문　06 (악기를) 다시 조율하다
07 발명하다　08 불가능한　09 금속　10 모이다
11 빛나다　12 발견하다; 알아내다　13 공연, 연주회
14 독특한　15 얼(리)다; 얼 정도로 춥게 느끼다
16 고대의　17 ~을 포함하여　18 싸다, 포장하다
19 창의력, 창조성　20 막다, 방지하다　21 성공
22 ~이긴 하지만　23 북부의, 북부에 위치한
24 performance　25 easily　26 melt
27 cheap　28 ship　29 trade　30 refrigerator
31 store　32 free　33 delicate　34 audience
35 impressive　36 string　37 pond
38 다양한, 여러 가지의　39 개최되다, 일어나다
40 ~을 생각해내다

VOCABULARY TEST 2

A ⓑ　B ⓑ　C 1 success　2 discover
3 creativity　4 gather　D 1 took place
2 variety of　3 come up with

GRAMMAR TEST

A 1 any secrets　2 something　3 clothes
　4 a lot of friends
B 1 money to take　2 homework to do
　3 to borrow some books　4 to buy some
　groceries
C 1 나는 너에게 말할 것이 있다.
　2 그는 대학교에 입학하기 위해 열심히 공부했다.
　3 그녀는 이메일을 확인하기 위해 컴퓨터를 켰다.
　4 제주도는 휴가를 즐기기에 좋은 장소이다.

WRITING TEST

A 1 free ice to try　2 Tudor tried to ship
　3 must be retuned
　4 each time they are played
　5 prevent the audience from freezing
B 1 are made of ice　2 to store the ice
　3 gather to hear　4 can be bought
　5 to take ice from

UNIT 10 | Competition pp. 38–41

VOCABULARY TEST 1

01 어리석은　02 소리치다　03 자랑하다, 떠벌리다
04 노 젓는 사람　05 지나가다　06 막대기　07 ~의
위험을 무릅쓰다　08 행동　09 노를 젓다
10 놀랍게도　11 허풍, 자랑　12 재능이 있는
13 (붙)잡다, 움켜잡다　14 보호하다, 지키다　15 바로
16 1인용의; (단) 하나의　17 가로지르다, 건너다
18 드러내다, 밝히다　19 (수)행하다　20 중반부에
21 소리치다　22 각각의　23 신기하게도
24 compete　25 punish　26 heroic
27 disguise　28 weave　29 goddess
30 opponent　31 lose　32 eventually
33 event　34 furious　35 picture
36 challenge　37 기록을 세우다　38 ~을 따라잡다
39 선두에 서다　40 ~ 앞에

VOCABULARY TEST 2

A ⓓ　B ⓒ　C 1 deed　2 brag　3 risk
4 punish　D 1 take the lead　2 in front of
3 catch up with

GRAMMAR TEST

A 1 to be　2 to study　3 to buy　4 opening
B 1 to see　2 looking　3 doing　4 to lose
C 1 avoid eating junk food
　2 gave up smoking
　3 enjoy watching movies
　4 promised to return my book

WRITING TEST

A 1 Was this talent given
　2 made Athena furious
　3 started to weave
　4 After the ducks had passed
　5 that there are more important
B 1 risked losing the race
　2 very talented at weaving
　3 decided to disguise herself
　4 kept rowing and took
　5 he was competing

UNIT 11 | Sea pp. 42-45

VOCABULARY TEST 1

01 항로, 경로 **02** ~ 이내에[안에] **03** 놓다, 두다; (알을) 낳다 **04** 놀라운 **05** 완전히, 충분히 **06** 야생, 자연 **07** 장어 **08** 깊이 **09** 성별 **10** 활발한, 왕성한 **11** 주요한 **12** 납작한; 평평한 **13** 선원 **14** 탐험하다 **15** 주변 환경 **16** 판명되다, 드러나다 **17** 놀랍게도 **18** 사실이 아닌, 허위의 **19** ~ 밑[아래]에 **20** 대양, 바다 **21** 고요(함), 평온(함) **22** 거대한 **23** 생산하다 **24** unfortunately **25** countless **26** appearance **27** male **28** creature **29** unfamiliar **30** female **31** voyage **32** discovery **33** wave **34** navigator **35** bright **36** adult **37** 태어나다 **38** ~을 우연히 발견하다[만나다] **39** ~에서 유래된[파생된] **40** ~까지

VOCABULARY TEST 2

A ⓒ B ⓑ C 1 voyage 2 discovery 3 lay 4 prove D 1 up to 2 came upon 3 derived from

GRAMMAR TEST

A 1 or 2 and 3 when 4 After
B 1 when 2 but 3 before 4 and
C 1 flour and milk
  2 cheap but tasty
  3 When I was young
  4 Before you have dinner

WRITING TEST

A 1 after it lays eggs
  2 It is not easy to find
  3 When it turns yellow
  4 came upon an unfamiliar ocean
  5 that would prove untrue
B 1 haven't explored
  2 As it gets bigger
  3 waving in the water
  4 the deepest and largest
  5 was given by

UNIT 12 | Environment pp. 46-49

VOCABULARY TEST 1

01 오염, 공해 **02** 돌아가다 **03** (절)반 **04** 반대의, 거꾸로 된; 뒤집다, 뒤바꾸다 **05** 바다, 대양 **06** 펼치다; 확산되다, 퍼지다 **07** 창의력 **08** 줄이다, 낮추다 **09** 표면, 지면 **10** 유형, 종류 **11** 인간, 인류 **12** 결과, 결실 **13** 공격하다 **14** 해변, 바닷가 **15** 벽 **16** 살아남다, 생존하다 **17** 부화하다 **18** 가능한 **19** 보통 **20** 해로운, 유해한 **21** 직물, 천; 재료 **22** 최근에 **23** predator **24** contrast **25** reach **26** last **27** adult **28** trend **29** breed **30** avoid **31** female **32** require **33** temporary **34** face **35** dolphin **36** 위험에 처한 **37** ~의 밖으로; ~ 중에 **38** ~로 나아가다 **39** 깨끗이 치우다 **40** ~로 알려진

VOCABULARY TEST 2

A ⓐ B ⓒ C 1 hatch 2 result 3 last 4 reach D 1 known as 2 in danger 3 made his way to

GRAMMAR TEST

A 1 if 2 Because 3 that 4 that
B 1 that 2 that 3 because 4 if
C 1 (만약) 눈이 많이 온다면, 그 행사는 취소될 것이다.
  2 그녀는 너무 열심히 일했기 때문에 매우 피곤했다.
  3 그의 의견은 모든 사람들이 게임에 참여해야 한다는 것이다.
  4 (만약) 네가 내일 일찍 일어나지 않는다면, 너는 학교에 늦을 것이다.

WRITING TEST

A 1 must make their way
  2 has been used as
  3 such as posters and leaflets
  4 half of them are eaten
  5 the number of surviving
B 1 has always been difficult
  2 making the problem much worse
  3 possible to create graffiti
  4 are made by
  5 known as clean graffiti

READING
Inside

Answer Key

A 4-level curriculum
integration reading course

- **A thematic reading program that integrates with school curriculum**
  중등 교육과정이 지향하는 문이과 통합 및 타교과 연계 반영한 독해서

- **Informative content with well-designed comprehension questions**
  정보성 있는 지문과 질 높은 다양한 유형의 문항 그리고 서술형 평가도 대비

- **Grammar points directly related to the *Grammar Inside* series**
  베스트셀러 Grammar Inside와 직접적으로 연계된 문법 항목 및 문항 제공

- **Exercises with useful, essential, and academic vocabulary**
  중등 필수 어휘 학습 코너 제공

- **A workbook for more vocabulary, grammar, and reading exercises**
  풍부한 양의 어휘, 문법, 그리고 쓰기 추가 문제 등을 수록한 워크북

Level	Grade	Words Limit
Reading Inside Starter	**Low-Intermediate**	**140-160**
Reading Inside Level 1	Intermediate	160-180
Reading Inside Level 2	Intermediate	180-200
Reading Inside Level 3	Low-Advanced	200-220

NE능률 교재 MAP

독해

초1-2	초3	초3-4	초4-5	초5-6
초등영어 리딩이 된다 Start 1	리딩버디 1	리딩버디 2	리딩버디 3	초등영어 리딩이 된다 Jump 1
초등영어 리딩이 된다 Start 2		초등영어 리딩이 된다 Basic 1	주니어 리딩튜터 스타터 1	초등영어 리딩이 된다 Jump 2
초등영어 리딩이 된다 Start 3		초등영어 리딩이 된다 Basic 2		초등영어 리딩이 된다 Jump 3
초등영어 리딩이 된다 Start 4		초등영어 리딩이 된다 Basic 3		초등영어 리딩이 된다 Jump 4
		초등영어 리딩이 된다 Basic 4		주니어 리딩튜터 스타터 2

초6-예비중	중1	중1-2	중2-3	중3
주니어 리딩튜터 1	1316 Reading 1	1316 Reading 2	1316 Reading 3	리딩튜터 입문
Junior Reading Expert 1	주니어 리딩튜터 2	주니어 리딩튜터 3	주니어 리딩튜터 4	정말 기특한 구문독해 완성
Reading Forward Basic 1	Junior Reading Expert 2	정말 기특한 구문독해 입문	정말 기특한 구문독해 기본	Reading Forward Advanced 1
	Reading Forward Basic 2	Junior Reading Expert 3	Junior Reading Expert 4	열중 16강 독해+문법 3
	열중 16강 독해+문법 1	Reading Forward Intermediate 1	Reading Forward Intermediate 2	Reading Inside 3
	Reading Inside Starter	열중 16강 독해+문법 2	Reading Inside 2	
		Reading Inside 1		

중3-예비고	고1	고1-2	고2-3, 수능 실전	고3 이상, 수능 고난도
Reading Expert 1	빠바 기초세우기	빠바 구문독해	빠바 유형독해	Reading Expert 5
리딩튜터 기본	리딩튜터 실력	리딩튜터 수능 PLUS	빠바 종합실전편	능률 고급영문독해
Reading Forward Advanced 2	Reading Expert 2	Reading Expert 3	Reading Expert 4	
	TEPS BY STEP G+R Basic		TEPS BY STEP G+R 1	

수능 이상/ 토플 80-89· 텝스 600-699점	수능 이상/ 토플 90-99· 텝스 700-799점	수능 이상/ 토플 100· 텝스 800점 이상
ADVANCED Reading Expert 1	ADVANCED Reading Expert 2	RADIX TOEFL Black Label Reading 2
TEPS BY STEP G+R 2	RADIX TOEFL Black Label Reading 1	TEPS BY STEP G+R 3
RADIX TOEFL Blue Label Reading 1, 2		

READING Inside

workbook

STARTER

A 4-level curriculum
integration reading course

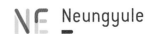

NE Neungyule

Workbook

READING
Inside

STARTER

반 / 이름:

[01–23] 다음 단어의 뜻을 쓰시오.

01 tradition _____

02 slavery _____

03 shipping _____

04 similar _____

05 heartbeat _____

06 nowadays _____

07 amazing _____

08 tone _____

09 modern _____

10 stick _____

11 begin _____

12 patent _____

13 performance _____

14 loud _____

15 impressive _____

16 instrument _____

17 spread _____

18 produce _____

19 inspire _____

20 clearly _____

21 eventually _____

22 hollow _____

23 rich _____

[24–35] 다음 뜻을 지닌 단어를 쓰시오.

24 상담하다 _____

25 그리워하다 _____

26 연안[해안]의 _____

27 붙잡다, 포획하다 _____

28 심장 _____

29 전자 장치를 쓰지 않는 _____

30 탄생, 출생 _____

31 아주 작은 _____

32 소리, 소음 _____

33 가슴, 흉부 _____

34 굵다 _____

35 금속 _____

[36–40] 다음 표현의 뜻을 쓰시오.

36 go for a walk _____

37 roll up _____

38 for free _____

39 plenty of _____

40 a range of _____

A 다음 영영 정의에 해당하는 단어를 고르시오.

> like somebody or something but not exactly the same

ⓐ creative   ⓑ similar   ⓒ modern   ⓓ different

B 다음 밑줄 친 단어와 비슷한 의미의 단어를 고르시오.

> I found a <u>tiny</u> hole in my sock.

ⓐ huge   ⓑ small   ⓒ quiet   ⓓ sick

C 다음 빈칸에 알맞은 단어를 보기에서 골라 쓰시오.

> 보기   impressive   instrument   noise   hollow

1 What kind of musical _____ can you play?

2 The singer's performance was very _____.

3 The _____ distracted me from my studying.

4 The statue is not heavy because it is _____.

D 다음 우리말과 일치하도록 빈칸에 알맞은 말을 쓰시오.

1 어두워지기 전에 산책하러 가자.

▶ Let's g_____ f_____ a w_____ before it gets dark.

2 그 슈퍼마켓은 다양한 유기농 제품들을 판다.

▶ The supermarket sells a r_____ o_____ organic products.

3 그는 소매를 둘둘 말고 화장실을 청소하기 시작했다.

▶ He r_____ u_____ his sleeves and started to clean the bathroom.

GRAMMAR TEST

A 다음 ( ) 안에서 알맞은 것을 고르시오.

1 They (meet / met) at the restaurant yesterday.

2 I didn't (make / made) any mistakes on the test.

3 She (writes / wrote) an email to me a month ago.

4 Did they (play / played) badminton this afternoon?

B 우리말과 일치하도록 보기 안의 동사를 이용하여 문장을 완성하시오.

보기	read	buy	break	drink

1 Tim은 어제 그 컵을 깼다.

▶ Tim _____ the cup yesterday.

2 나는 열 살 때 그 소설을 읽었다.

▶ I _____ the novel when I was ten.

3 그는 일주일 전에 새 자전거를 샀다.

▶ He _____ a new bicycle a week ago.

4 Sally는 오늘 아침에 커피 한 잔을 마셨다.

▶ Sally _____ a cup of coffee this morning.

C 우리말과 일치하도록 ( ) 안에 주어진 말을 바르게 배열하시오.

1 너는 그 액션 영화를 즐겼니? (did / enjoy / you)

▶ _____ the action movie?

2 그는 어젯밤에 피아노를 치지 않았다. (didn't / he / play)

▶ _____ the piano last night.

3 내 아빠는 어제 세차하지 않으셨다. (didn't / clean / my dad)

▶ _____ his car yesterday.

4 그들은 동물원으로 현장학습을 갔니? (did / go / they)

▶ _____ on a field trip to the zoo?

A 우리말과 일치하도록 ( ) 안에 주어진 말을 바르게 배열하시오.

1 그들은 더는 드럼을 갖고 있지 않았다. (have / didn't / drums / they)

▶ _____ anymore.

2 카혼은 많은 종류의 현대 음악에서 사용된다. (used / is / many kinds / in)

▶ The cajon _____ of modern music.

3 René Laennec이라는 이름의 프랑스 의사는 산책하러 갔다.

(named / went / René Laennec / for)

▶ A French doctor _____ a walk.

4 관 형태의 그 막대기가 아주 작은 소리를 매우 크게 만들고 있었다!

(the tiny noise / very loud / making)

▶ The tube-shaped stick was _____!

5 많은 서아프리카인들은 붙잡혀서 미대륙으로 끌려갔다.

(captured / brought / and / were)

▶ Many West Africans _____ to the Americas.

B 우리말과 일치하도록 ( ) 안의 말을 이용하여 문장을 완성하시오.

1 그는 관을 만들기 위해 종이 한 장을 말았다. (make, a tube)

▶ He rolled up a piece of paper _____ _____ _____ _____.

2 그는 이 아이디어에 의해 영감을 받았다. (inspire, by, this idea)

▶ He was _____ _____ _____ _____.

3 이것이 그들로 하여금 드럼을 연주하는 것을 막았을까? (them, from, drum)

▶ Did this stop _____ _____ _____?

4 그는 두 소년이 속이 빈 막대를 가지고 놀고 있는 것을 보았다. (see, two boys, play)

▶ He _____ _____ _____ with a hollow stick.

5 그들은 그 상자들을 드럼처럼 연주하기로 했다. (decide, play, the crates)

▶ They _____ _____ _____ _____ _____ like drums.

VOCABULARY TEST 1

반 / 이름:

[01-23] 다음 단어의 뜻을 쓰시오.

01 run _____

02 every _____

03 pay _____

04 choose _____

05 product _____

06 hire _____

07 exactly _____

08 household _____

09 low _____

10 fact _____

11 price _____

12 business _____

13 encourage _____

14 global _____

15 medicine _____

16 employee _____

17 imagine _____

18 ambition _____

19 consumer _____

20 huge _____

21 commonly _____

22 method _____

23 customer _____

[24-35] 다음 뜻을 지닌 단어를 쓰시오.

24 전 세계에 걸쳐 _____

25 속이다 _____

26 제시[제출]하다 _____

27 대중의 _____

28 결정, 판단 _____

29 비싼, 돈이 많이 드는 _____

30 하인, 고용인 _____

31 확산, 전파 _____

32 (값·비용이) ~이다 _____

33 옳은 일; 권리, 권한 _____

34 저렴한, 돈이 적게 드는 _____

35 획기[혁신]적인 _____

[36-40] 다음 표현의 뜻을 쓰시오.

36 on one's behalf _____

37 come up with _____

38 have a cold _____

39 out of _____

40 have an effect on _____

A 다음 영영 정의에 해당하는 단어를 고르시오.

> a strong desire to achieve something

ⓐ product   ⓑ price   ⓒ ambition   ⓓ business

B 다음 밑줄 친 단어와 비슷한 의미의 단어를 고르시오.

> This <u>method</u> of making cookies is very simple.

ⓐ reason   ⓑ amount   ⓒ way   ⓓ item

C 다음 빈칸에 알맞은 단어를 보기에서 골라 쓰시오.

> 보기   right   hire   encourage   decision

1 Most doctors _____ people to exercise.

2 Everyone has the _____ to be treated equally.

3 They have to make a final _____ before this Friday.

4 The company is going to _____ new staff members.

D 다음 우리말과 일치하도록 빈칸에 알맞은 말을 쓰시오.

1 향은 우리의 기분에 영향을 미친다.

  ▶ Scents h_____ a_____ e_____ o_____ our feelings.

2 그는 깡통을 재활용할 새로운 아이디어를 내놓았다.

  ▶ He c_____ u_____ w_____ a new idea for recycling cans.

3 너의 부모님 중 한 분이 너를 대신해서 서식에 서명할 수 있다.

  ▶ One of your parents can sign the form o_____ y_____ b_____.

A 다음 ( ) 안에서 알맞은 것을 고르시오.

1 Your voice sounds (strange / strangely).

2 The song made my brother (sad / sadly).

3 Jane looks (beautiful / beautifully) today.

4 My friends call (a bookworm me / me a bookworm).

B 다음 문장의 밑줄 친 부분을 바르게 고치시오.

1 This box feels <u>heavily</u>. _____

2 The candy tastes <u>sweetly</u>. _____

3 Her smile made me <u>happily</u>. _____

4 He always keeps <u>clean his room</u>. _____

5 The movie made <u>a famous actress her</u>. _____

C 다음 문장을 우리말로 옮기시오.

1 The flowers smell nice.

▶ _____

2 This sweater feels soft.

▶ _____

3 The movie made me sad.

▶ _____

4 The mug kept the tea warm.

▶ _____

A 우리말과 일치하도록 (   ) 안에 주어진 말을 바르게 배열하시오.

1 당신은 조금의 약을 사고 싶다. (buy / want / you / to)

▶ _____ some medicine.

2 이것이 Martha의 미용실을 크게 성공하게 했다. (made / this / Martha's salon)

▶ _____ a huge success.

3 일 년에 350달러인 회원권은 너무 비싸게 들릴지도 모른다. (too / sound / expensive / might)

▶ A membership that costs $350 a year _____.

4 그녀는 자기 자신의 사업을 위한 돈을 모으려고 25년 동안 일했다. (to / money / save / for)

▶ She worked for 25 years _____ her own business.

5 마케팅 담당자들은 그들의 상품에 대한 사실이 더 좋게 들리게 하려고 그것을 사용한다.

(their products / sound / facts / about)

▶ Marketers use it to make _____ better.

B 우리말과 일치하도록 (   ) 안의 말을 이용하여 문장을 완성하시오.

1 그것은 훨씬 더 저렴하게 들린다. (sound, much, cheap)

▶ It _____ _____ _____.

2 Martha는 종업원을 고용하고 싶지 않았다. (want, hire)

▶ Martha _____ _____ _____ _____ employees.

3 그녀의 고객들은 Martha가 더 많은 미용실을 열도록 권했다. (encourage, Martha, open)

▶ Her customers _____ _____ _____ _____ more salons.

4 Martha는 자신의 미용실 이름을 사용할 권리를 팔았다. (the right, use)

▶ Martha sold _____ _____ _____ _____ the name of her salon.

5 Martha에게서 보수를 받는 대신, 그 여성들은 그들 자신의 Harper's Salon을 운영했다.

(instead, of, be, pay)

▶ _____ _____ _____ _____ by Martha, the women ran their own

Harper's Salons.

VOCABULARY TEST 1

[01-23] 다음 단어의 뜻을 쓰시오.

01 duty _____

02 skillfully _____

03 aircraft _____

04 complete _____

05 technician _____

06 plane _____

07 prepared _____

08 journey _____

09 remove _____

10 distance _____

11 spray _____

12 contact _____

13 lighting _____

14 cool _____

15 handle _____

16 thick _____

17 alone _____

18 temperature _____

19 carefully _____

20 thin _____

21 humidity _____

22 enable _____

23 dust _____

[24-35] 다음 뜻을 지닌 단어를 쓰시오.

24 운동선수 _____

25 층, 겹; 층층이 쌓다 _____

26 (날씨 등의) 상태 _____

27 무사히, 안전하게 _____

28 조종사, 비행사 _____

29 예상치 못한, 예상 밖의 _____

30 영향을 미치다 _____

31 복잡한 _____

32 수행하다; (경기 등을) 하다 _____

33 비행, 여행; 항공기 _____

34 응급 (상황) _____

35 착륙하다, 내려앉다 _____

[36-40] 다음 표현의 뜻을 쓰시오.

36 take off _____

37 one another _____

38 thousands of _____

39 at a time _____

40 take care of _____

A 다음 영영 정의에 해당하는 단어를 고르시오.

> communication with a person, especially by talking or writing to them frequently

ⓐ emergency   ⓑ athlete   ⓒ temperature   ⓓ contact

B 다음 밑줄 친 단어와 비슷한 의미의 단어를 고르시오.

> We have to work together to complete the project.

ⓐ start   ⓑ finish   ⓒ allow   ⓓ stop

C 다음 빈칸에 알맞은 단어를 보기에서 골라 쓰시오.

> 보기   remove   hurt   unexpected   complicated

1 I was surprised by her _____ visit.

2 My shoes are too tight, so they _____ my toes.

3 You should _____ the green tops from the carrots.

4 His explanation sounded so _____. Nobody understood it.

D 다음 우리말과 일치하도록 빈칸에 알맞은 말을 쓰시오.

1 비행기가 곧 이륙할 것이다.
   ▶ The airplane will t_____ o_____ soon.

2 그 아이는 한 번에 두 계단씩 뛰어 올라갔다.
   ▶ The kid ran up the stairs two a_____ a t_____.

3 수많은 사람들이 바다에서 수영을 하고 있었다.
   ▶ T_____ o_____ people were swimming in the sea.

A 다음 빈칸에 알맞은 것을 보기에서 골라 쓰시오.

> 보기 showed   asked   to save   to clean   to finish   to come

1 My brother _____ me a favor.

2 He ordered them _____ the room.

3 The painter _____ me her paintings.

4 I wanted you _____ to my birthday party.

5 The new plan allowed them _____ a lot of time.

6 They expected you _____ the work before five o'clock.

B 우리말과 일치하도록 (   ) 안에 주어진 말을 바르게 배열하시오.

1 그녀는 그에게 그 파일들을 이메일로 보냈다. (sent / the files / him)
  ▶ She _____ by email.

2 그 선생님은 나에게 약간의 조언을 해줬다. (gave / some advice / me)
  ▶ The teacher _____.

3 그 의사는 나에게 물을 많이 마시라고 말했다. (to drink / told / me)
  ▶ The doctor _____ lots of water.

4 나는 그녀에게 그 제안을 수락할 것을 조언했다. (her / advised / to accept)
  ▶ I _____ the offer.

5 그들은 그녀에게 테니스 동아리에 가입하기를 요청했다. (asked / to join / her)
  ▶ They _____ the tennis club.

6 Kathy는 지난 일요일에 나에게 책들을 빌려줬다. (me / some books / lent)
  ▶ Kathy _____ last Sunday.

7 우리 아빠는 나에게 직접 새 의자를 만들어 주셨다. (a new chair / me / made)
  ▶ My dad _____ by himself.

A 우리말과 일치하도록 ( ) 안에 주어진 말을 바르게 배열하시오.

1 그들에게는, 얼음이 더 두껍고 덜 차가워야 한다. (be / cold / less / thicker / and)
  ▶ For them, the ice should _____.

2 그들은 그런 얼음 위에서 점프하면 다칠 것이다. (hurt / from / jumping / themselves)
  ▶ They would _____ on that ice.

3 그들은 조종사에게 기상 상태와 같은 정보를 제공한다. (the pilot / information / give)
  ▶ They _____ such as weather conditions.

4 항공 운항 관제사는 항공기가 착륙하는 것을 도울 수 있다. (help / one aircraft / might / land)
  ▶ An air traffic controller _____.

5 항공 운항 관제사들은 반드시 비행기들이 서로 안전거리를 유지하도록 한다.
  (make / that / sure / the planes)
  ▶ Air traffic controllers _____ keep a safe distance
  between one another.

B 우리말과 일치하도록 ( ) 안의 말을 이용하여 문장을 완성하시오.

1 조종사는 한 번에 한 대의 항공기를 책임진다. (responsible)
  ▶ A pilot _____ _____ _____ one flight at a time.

2 좋은 얼음은 선수들이 안전하게 경기할 수 있게 합니다. (enable, athletes, perform)
  ▶ Good ice _____ _____ _____ _____ safely.

3 어떻게 좋은 얼음은 스케이트 선수들이 더 잘 경기하게 할까? (allow, skaters, perform)
  ▶ How does good ice _____ _____ _____ _____ better?

4 안전한 여행을 하기 위해서는 많은 사람들이 필요하다. (be, need, make)
  ▶ Many people _____ _____ _____ _____ a safe journey.

5 얼음의 온도와 두께를 조절하는 것이 중요하다. (it, important, adjust)
  ▶ _____ _____ _____ _____ the ice's temperature and thickness.

UNIT 04 | Technology

[01-23] 다음 단어의 뜻을 쓰시오.

01 result _____

02 sensor _____

03 create _____

04 street _____

05 bin _____

06 decision _____

07 eco-friendly _____

08 neighborhood _____

09 signal _____

10 corner _____

11 several _____

12 totally _____

13 high-tech _____

14 instrument _____

15 dangerous _____

16 warn _____

17 free _____

18 area _____

19 forecast _____

20 already _____

21 expect _____

22 data _____

23 information _____

[24-35] 다음 뜻을 지닌 단어를 쓰시오.

24 이전의 _____

25 날씨 _____

26 접근; 접속 _____

27 비교하다 _____

28 두다, 놓다 _____

29 고도로, 매우 _____

30 붙잡다, 움켜잡다 _____

31 찌부러뜨리다, 눌러 부수다 _____

32 정확한 _____

33 발달[진보]한 _____

34 수집품; 수거, 수집 _____

35 처리하다 _____

[36-40] 다음 표현의 뜻을 쓰시오.

36 see into _____

37 afford to _____

38 give out _____

39 put on _____

40 tons of _____

A 다음 영영 정의에 해당하는 단어를 고르시오.

> to press something so hard that it is damaged or loses its shape

ⓐ grab   ⓑ place   ⓒ crush   ⓓ compare

B 다음 밑줄 친 단어와 반대 의미의 단어를 고르시오.

> The information in the newspaper was accurate.

ⓐ simple   ⓑ safe   ⓒ traditional   ⓓ false

C 다음 빈칸에 알맞은 단어를 보기 에서 골라 쓰시오.

> 보기   free   bin   previous   dangerous

1 It's _____ to drive carelessly.

2 Admission to this museum is _____.

3 The character appeared in the _____ chapter.

4 Don't forget to empty the _____ when it gets full.

D 다음 우리말과 일치하도록 빈칸에 알맞은 말을 쓰시오.

1 그는 새 차를 살 형편이 안 된다.
   ▶ He can't a_____ t_____ buy a new car.

2 당신은 사람의 마음을 들여다볼 수 없다.
   ▶ You can't s_____ i_____ a person's mind.

3 그 벽난로는 많은 열을 발산한다.
   ▶ The fireplace g_____ o_____ a lot of heat.

A 다음 ( ) 안에서 알맞은 것을 고르시오.

1 I'm short. I (can / can't) reach the shelf.

2 (Can / Must) you help me with something?

3 To finish this project, we (must / must not) work together.

4 We (have to / don't have to) hurry. The lesson will start soon.

B 다음 문장의 밑줄 친 부분을 우리말로 옮기시오.

1 You <u>don't have to pay</u> the extra fee.

▶ _____

2 They <u>must not park</u> in front of the entrance.

▶ _____

3 His arm is broken. He <u>cannot write</u> a letter now.

▶ _____

C 우리말과 일치하도록 ( ) 안의 말을 이용하여 문장을 완성하시오.

1 너는 그녀를 기다릴 필요가 없다. (wait, for, her)

▶ You _____ .

2 그들은 학교 규칙을 따라야 한다. (follow, the school rules)

▶ They _____ .

3 Alicia는 4개 국어를 말할 수 있다. (speak, four languages)

▶ Alicia _____ .

4 당신은 항상 여권을 가지고 다녀야 한다. (carry, your passport)

▶ You _____ all the time.

A 우리말과 일치하도록 ( ) 안에 주어진 말을 바르게 배열하시오.

1 새로운 무언가가 도시의 거리로 오고 있다. (new / something / coming / is)

▶ _____ to city streets.

2 스마트 쓰레기통은 동네를 더 좋게 만든다. (better / neighborhood / makes / a)

▶ A smart bin _____.

3 일기 예보는 우리에게 날씨에 대한 예측을 제공한다. (us / give / predictions)

▶ Weather forecasts _____ about the weather.

4 그들은 기상 관측소에서 나온 수많은 양의 정보를 이용해야 한다. (use / have / tons / of / to)

▶ They _____ information from weather stations.

5 가장 놀라운 것은 각각의 스마트 쓰레기통이 와이파이 핫스팟이라는 점이다.

(each / that / is / smart bin)

▶ The most amazing thing is _____ a Wi-Fi hotspot.

B 우리말과 일치하도록 ( ) 안의 말을 이용하여 문장을 완성하시오.

1 오늘 비가 올 것이다. (rain)

▶ It's _____ _____ _____ today.

2 많은 사람들이 매일 인터넷을 사용하는 것을 즐긴다. (enjoy, use, the internet)

▶ Many people _____ _____ _____ _____ every day.

3 일기 예보는 기상학자라고 불리는 사람들에 의해 만들어진다. (create, by, people)

▶ Weather forecasts _____ _____ _____ _____ called
meteorologists.

4 일부 사람들은 인터넷 접속을 위한 비용을 지불할 형편이 안 된다. (can, afford, pay)

▶ Some people _____ _____ _____ _____ for internet access.

5 그들은 결과와 이전의 날씨 패턴을 비교하여 예측할 수 있다. (compare, the results)

▶ They _____ _____ _____ _____ _____ previous weather
patterns to make their predictions.

VOCABULARY TEST 1

반 / 이름:

[01-23] 다음 단어의 뜻을 쓰시오.

01 material _____

02 trash _____

03 capital _____

04 unusual _____

05 local _____

06 advertisement _____

07 absorb _____

08 float _____

09 pollution _____

10 collect _____

11 store _____

12 present _____

13 increase _____

14 create _____

15 purify _____

16 remove _____

17 harbor _____

18 suck _____

19 tap _____

20 weapon _____

21 heavy _____

22 provide _____

23 below _____

[24-35] 다음 뜻을 지닌 단어를 쓰시오.

24 붙이다 _____

25 사막 _____

26 교통(량), 차량들 _____

27 (옥외의 커다란) 광고판 _____

28 천연[자연]의 _____

29 달리다; 작동하다 _____

30 풀어주다; 방출하다 _____

31 여과하다, 거르다 _____

32 목이 마른, 갈증이 난 _____

33 효과적인 _____

34 대기 _____

35 일단 ~하면 _____

[36-40] 다음 표현의 뜻을 쓰시오.

36 made of _____

37 take in _____

38 due to _____

39 by oneself _____

40 set up _____

A 다음 영영 정의에 해당하는 단어를 고르시오.

to take in a gas, liquid, or other substance

ⓐ absorb   ⓑ filter   ⓒ release   ⓓ increase

B 다음 밑줄 친 단어와 비슷한 의미의 단어를 고르시오.

The aquarium has many <u>unusual</u> tropical fish.

ⓐ unique   ⓑ light   ⓒ little   ⓓ global

C 다음 빈칸에 알맞은 단어를 보기 에서 골라 쓰시오.

보기   float   desert   store   weapon

1 A knife is a kind of _____.

2 It is hard to find water in the _____.

3 Some animals _____ up food for the winter.

4 These plants can _____ on the surface of the water.

D 다음 우리말과 일치하도록 빈칸에 알맞은 말을 쓰시오.

1 John은 그의 차를 혼자 힘으로 고쳤다.

   ▶ John fixed his car b_____ h_____.

2 그 축구 경기는 폭우 때문에 취소되었다.

   ▶ The soccer game was canceled d_____ t_____ heavy rain.

3 그는 캠핑장에 도착하여 텐트를 치기 시작했다.

   ▶ He arrived at the camping site and started to s_____ u_____ the tent.

A 다음 ( ) 안에서 알맞은 것을 고르시오.

1 (Watch / Watching) SF movies is interesting.

2 He practices (play / playing) the piano every day.

3 My dream is (meet / meeting) the singer in person.

4 Wendy's goal is (passing / passed) this math exam.

B 우리말과 일치하도록 보기 안의 동사를 이용하여 문장을 완성하시오.

| 보기 | get | eat | run |

1 나는 아침 식사를 하고 있다.
  ▶ I _____ _____ breakfast.

2 바깥이 어두워지고 있다.
  ▶ It _____ _____ dark outside.

3 그들은 강을 따라 달리고 있다.
  ▶ They _____ _____ along the river.

C 우리말과 일치하도록 ( ) 안의 말을 이용하여 문장을 완성하시오.

1 나의 직업은 스페인어를 가르치는 것이다. (teach, Spanish)
  ▶ My job is _____ _____.

2 그는 그의 두 마리의 개를 산책시키는 중이다. (he, walk)
  ▶ _____ _____ _____ his two dogs.

3 그녀는 지금 무대 위에서 춤을 추고 있다. (she, dance)
  ▶ _____ _____ _____ on the stage now.

4 탄산음료를 많이 마시는 것은 너의 치아에 좋지 않다. (drink, too much, soda)
  ▶ _____ _____ _____ _____ is not good for your teeth.

A 우리말과 일치하도록 ( ) 안에 주어진 말을 바르게 배열하시오.

1 그 도시는 사막에 있다. (located / in / is / a desert)

▶ The city _____.

2 그 광고판은 매일 90리터가 넘는 물을 모은다. (than / 90 liters / more / of water)

▶ The billboard collects _____ every day.

3 그것은 쓰레기를 없애기 위해 호주의 서퍼들에 의해 발명되었다. (invented / was / by / it)

▶ _____ Australian surfers to remove trash.

4 그것은 천연 재료로 만들어진 그물 주머니를 내부에 가지고 있다. (of / materials / natural / made)

▶ It has a mesh bag inside _____.

5 한 대학이 이러한 문제에 맞서 싸우기 위해 독특한 무기를 만들었다. (problems / fight / these / to)

▶ A university has created an unusual weapon _____.

B 우리말과 일치하도록 ( ) 안의 말을 이용하여 문장을 완성하시오.

1 Seabin은 물에 떠 있는 쓰레기통이다. (float, garbage bin)

▶ The Seabin is a _____ _____ _____.

2 극심한 교통량으로 대기 오염 물질이 증가하고 있다. (increase)

▶ Air pollution _____ _____ due to heavy traffic.

3 Seabin을 바다 한 가운데에서 사용하는 것은 가능하지 않다. (use, the Seabin)

▶ _____ _____ _____ in open water isn't possible.

4 그 광고판은 여전히 광고로 사용된다. (be, still, use, as)

▶ The billboards _____ _____ _____ _____ advertisements.

5 그것은 Seabin이 물에서 기름을 제거하는 것을 가능하게 할 것이다! (remove, oil, from)

▶ It will allow the Seabin _____ _____ _____ _____ from the water!

VOCABULARY TEST 1

반 / 이름:

[01-23] 다음 단어의 뜻을 쓰시오.

01 diet _____

02 exactly _____

03 leftover _____

04 extra _____

05 participate _____

06 happen _____

07 smoke _____

08 partner _____

09 proper _____

10 slogan _____

11 nearby _____

12 choose _____

13 example _____

14 case _____

15 suggest _____

16 meal _____

17 charity _____

18 human _____

19 item _____

20 graduate _____

21 found _____

22 honey _____

23 simple _____

[24-37] 다음 뜻을 지닌 단어를 쓰시오.

24 함께 하다 _____

25 기부[기증]하다 _____

26 (비용·대가가) 들다; 비용 _____

27 편리한, 간편한 _____

28 혜택, 이득; 이익을 얻다 _____

29 관계 _____

30 돌려주다; 대답하다 _____

31 진정시키다 _____

32 따라가다 _____

33 협력하다 _____

34 안내하다 _____

35 단체, 조직 _____

36 늘어나다, 커지다 _____

37 (새·동물의) 울음소리 _____

[38-40] 다음 표현의 뜻을 쓰시오.

38 thanks to _____

39 call out _____

40 in need _____

VOCABULARY TEST 2

A 다음 영영 정의에 해당하는 단어를 고르시오.

> to work together with somebody else in order to achieve something

ⓐ cooperate ⓑ return ⓒ follow ⓓ found

B 다음 밑줄 친 단어와 비슷한 의미의 단어를 고르시오.

> A car accident can <u>happen</u> to anyone.

ⓐ help ⓑ occur ⓒ find ⓓ study

C 다음 빈칸에 알맞은 단어를 보기에서 골라 쓰시오.

> 보기 choose guide meals relationship

1 You should not skip your _____.

2 I will _____ you to the hotel room.

3 She has a close _____ with her aunt.

4 You have to _____ between the two choices.

D 다음 우리말과 일치하도록 빈칸에 알맞은 말을 쓰시오.

1 그는 어려움에 처한 많은 사람들을 도와왔다.
　▶ He has helped a lot of people i_____ n_____.

2 싱크대를 고치기 위해서, 우리는 배관공을 불러야 한다.
　▶ To fix the sink, we need to c_____ o_____ a plumber.

3 당신의 도움 덕분에, 나는 이 프로젝트를 끝낼 수 있었다.
　▶ T_____ t_____ your help, I was able to finish this project.

GRAMMAR TEST

A 다음 ( ) 안에서 알맞은 것을 고르시오.

1 My room is as (big / bigger) as yours.

2 Today's weather is as nice (as / than) yesterday's.

3 He bought red gloves. I bought black (one / ones).

4 Look at my new cell phone! I bought (it / one) last week.

B 다음 빈칸에 알맞은 단어를 보기 에서 골라 쓰시오.

> 보기   it   they   one   ones

1 His chair is too old. He needs a new _____.

2 Look at those baby shoes! _____ look very cute.

3 I'm looking for pants. Do you have green _____?

4 Did you find your watch? – No, I haven't found _____ yet.

C 두 문장이 같은 의미가 되도록 ( ) 안의 말과 「as＋형용사/부사＋as」를 이용하여 문장을 완성하시오.

1 James is 15 years old. Amy is 15 years old too. (old)
  ▶ James is _____.

2 This coffee is 80°C. That tea is 80°C too. (hot)
  ▶ This coffee is _____.

3 This pine tree is 50 m tall. That oak tree is 50 m tall too. (tall)
  ▶ This pine tree is _____.

4 This train can go 100 kph. That car can go 100 kph too. (fast)
  ▶ This train can go _____.

반 / 이름:

A 우리말과 일치하도록 ( ) 안에 주어진 말을 바르게 배열하시오.

1 부수어서 열기에 어려운 것들도 있다. (hard / that / ones / are)

▶ There are _____ to break open.

2 그것은 식당에서 식사를 하는 것만큼 간단할 수 있다. (as / as / eating / simple)

▶ It can be _____ a meal at a restaurant.

3 그 돈은 어려움에 처한 누군가에게 식사를 제공하는 데 쓰인다. (give / meal / used / a / to)

▶ The money is _____ to someone in need.

4 그들은 꿀잡이새와 협력하는 사람들의 좋은 예이다. (with / cooperate / who / honeyguides)

▶ They are a great example of people _____.

5 Mealshare라는 이름의 한 자선 단체가 당신으로 하여금 바로 이것을 하게 한다.

(you / Mealshare / named / lets)

▶ A charity organization _____ do exactly this.

B 우리말과 일치하도록 ( ) 안의 말을 이용하여 문장을 완성하시오.

1 그 수는 계속 늘어나고 있다! (the number, keep, grow)

▶ _____ _____ _____ _____!

2 꿀잡이새라고 불리는 새들은 인간과 함께 일한다. (birds, call, honeyguides)

▶ _____ _____ _____ work with humans.

3 Mealshare는 캐나다에서 경영 대학원 졸업생들에 의해 설립되었다. (Mealshare, be, found)

▶ _____ _____ _____ in Canada by business school graduates.

4 어떤 동물들은 다른 동물들과 특별한 관계를 맺는 것으로부터 이익을 얻는다.

(have, a, special, relationship)

▶ Some animals benefit from _____ _____ _____ _____ with

other animals.

5 어려움에 처한 누군가를 돕는 것에 항상 추가의 시간이나 돈이 드는 것은 아니다.

(help, someone, in need)

▶ _____ _____ _____ _____ doesn't always have to cost you

extra time or money.

VOCABULARY TEST 1

반 / 이름:

[01-23] 다음 단어의 뜻을 쓰시오.

01 shape _____

02 touch _____

03 place _____

04 opponent _____

05 grass _____

06 lose _____

07 popularity _____

08 middle _____

09 push _____

10 metal _____

11 effect _____

12 gain _____

13 simple _____

14 substitute _____

15 signal _____

16 instead _____

17 rule _____

18 original _____

19 wooden _____

20 picture _____

21 react _____

22 popularity _____

23 underwater _____

[24-36] 다음 뜻을 지닌 단어를 쓰시오.

24 (절)반; 전반[후반] _____

25 (소리가) 울리다 _____

26 득점하다 _____

27 참가자 _____

28 ~ 동안 _____

29 야기하다, 초래하다 _____

30 여행하다; 이동하다 _____

31 직업의, 전문적인 _____

32 부드러운 _____

33 ~보다 위에[위로] _____

34 (공 등을) 튀게 하다; 튀다 _____

35 단단한 _____

36 골대, 골문 _____

[37-40] 다음 표현의 뜻을 쓰시오.

37 hold one's breath _____

38 hit a home run _____

39 made of _____

40 spring back _____

A 다음 영영 정의에 해당하는 단어를 고르시오.

> to win points, goals, etc., in a game or competition

ⓐ touch   ⓑ score   ⓒ push   ⓓ lose

B 다음 밑줄 친 단어와 비슷한 의미의 단어를 고르시오.

> The singer started to gain popularity in England.

ⓐ give   ⓑ put   ⓒ increase   ⓓ move

C 다음 빈칸에 알맞은 단어를 보기에서 골라 쓰시오.

> 보기   react   half   signal   opponent

1 They divided the pie in _____.

2 He pinched her, but she didn't _____.

3 When I give you the _____, you should run.

4 The boxer knocked his _____ down in the first round.

D 다음 우리말과 일치하도록 빈칸에 알맞은 말을 쓰시오.

1 그 탁자는 소나무로 만들어졌다.
   ▶ The table is m_____ o_____ pine tree.

2 딸꾹질이 날 때, 숨을 참으려고 노력해봐라.
   ▶ When you have hiccups, try to h_____ y_____ b_____.

3 그가 홈런을 쳤고, 관중들은 소리를 지르기 시작했다.
   ▶ He h_____ a h_____ r_____, and the crowd started screaming.

반 / 이름:

A 다음 ( ) 안에서 알맞은 것을 고르시오.

1 My muffin is (biger / bigger) than yours.

2 My sister sings (well / better) than my mother.

3 This red bag is (heavyer / heavier) than the black one.

4 The book is (interestinger / more interesting) than the movie.

B 밑줄 친 부분을 어법에 맞게 고쳐 쓰시오.

1 This plant grew more slowly <u>in</u> other plants. _____

2 The bakery is farther away <u>as</u> the supermarket. _____

3 This math test was <u>difficulter</u> than the previous one. _____

4 I think playing the violin is <u>more hard</u> than playing the piano. _____

C 우리말과 일치하도록 보기 안의 단어를 이용하여 문장을 완성하시오.

보기	high	bad	wise	fast

1 그 개는 그 울타리보다 더 높게 뛸 수 있다.
   ▶ The dog can jump _____ _____ the fence.

2 내 남동생은 그의 친구들보다 더 빨리 달릴 수 있다.
   ▶ My brother can run _____ _____ his friends.

3 오늘의 날씨는 지난 주보다 더 나쁘다.
   ▶ Today's weather is _____ _____ last week's.

4 그 노인은 마을의 다른 사람들보다 더 지혜롭다.
   ▶ The old man is _____ _____ the other people in town.

A 우리말과 일치하도록 ( ) 안에 주어진 말을 바르게 배열하시오.

1 이것은 공이 더 멀리 나아가게 한다. (farther / the ball / go / makes)
▶ This _____.

2 그것은 부드러운 잔디 위에서 공이 튀어 오르게 하는 것과 같다. (bouncing / like / a ball)
▶ It's _____ on soft grass.

3 경기 전에, 퍽은 수영장 중앙에 놓인다. (placed / the middle / in / is)
▶ Before the game, the puck _____ of the pool.

4 만약 그의 방망이가 금속이면, 공은 200미터보다 더 이동할 것이다! (travel / than / more / will)
▶ If his bat is metal, the ball _____ 200 meters!

5 다음에 하키를 하고 싶을 때는, 대신 수영장에 가 봐라. (you / to / want / next time)
▶ _____ play hockey, go to a swimming pool instead.

B 우리말과 일치하도록 ( ) 안의 말을 이용하여 문장을 완성하시오.

1 그 스틱은 아이스하키 스틱보다 더 짧다 (are, short)
▶ These sticks _____ _____ _____ ice hockey sticks.

2 이는 그것이 아이스하키보다 더 안전하기 때문이다. (it, is, safe)
▶ This is because _____ _____ _____ _____ ice hockey.

3 만약 그가 나무 방망이를 사용하면, 공은 약 150미터를 날아갈 것이다. (if, he, use)
▶ _____ _____ _____ a wooden bat, the ball will fly about 150 meters.

4 이는 공이 운동 에너지의 일부를 잃게 한다. (cause, the ball, lose)
▶ This _____ _____ _____ _____ _____ some of its kinetic energy.

5 심지어 70대인 선수들이 있다는 것을 들으면 당신은 놀랄지도 모른다. (surprised, hear)
▶ You might be _____ _____ _____ _____ there are even players in their 70s.

VOCABULARY TEST 1

반 / 이름:

[01–23] 다음 단어의 뜻을 쓰시오.

01 top _____

02 dry _____

03 Earth _____

04 goal _____

05 another _____

06 strange _____

07 usually _____

08 below _____

09 familiar _____

10 actually _____

11 extreme _____

12 perspective _____

13 publish _____

14 rich _____

15 sandy _____

16 country _____

17 desert _____

18 define _____

19 mistake _____

20 map _____

21 valuable _____

22 plant _____

23 area _____

[24–35] 다음 뜻을 지닌 단어를 쓰시오.

24 전형적인 _____

25 설명, 기술, 서술 _____

26 온도, 기온 _____

27 고정관념 _____

28 중요성 _____

29 다르게 _____

30 습기, 수분 _____

31 들어맞다 _____

32 맨 아래 (부분) _____

33 특징 _____

34 남극 (대륙) _____

35 집중하다 _____

[36–40] 다음 표현의 뜻을 쓰시오.

36 full of _____

37 tired of _____

38 come from _____

39 instead of _____

40 add to _____

A 다음 영영 정의에 해당하는 단어를 고르시오.

> a way of thinking about something

ⓐ perspective   ⓑ goal   ⓒ characteristic   ⓓ description

B 다음 밑줄 친 단어와 반대 의미의 단어를 고르시오.

> Kimchi is a typical Korean side dish.

ⓐ old   ⓑ common   ⓒ poor   ⓓ unique

C 다음 빈칸에 알맞은 단어를 보기에서 골라 쓰시오.

> 보기   extreme   mistake   publish   define

1 His _____ was due to inexperience.

2 We will _____ the novel next month.

3 I'm working under _____ pressure now.

4 It is hard to _____ the concept of beauty.

D 다음 우리말과 일치하도록 빈칸에 알맞은 말을 쓰시오.

1 나는 네 불평을 듣는 것에 싫증난다.
   ▶ I am t_____ o_____ listening to your complaints.

2 그 바구니는 사과와 오렌지로 가득 차 있다.
   ▶ The basket is f_____ o_____ apples and oranges.

3 젓가락을 사용하는 대신에, 너는 포크를 사용할 수 있다.
   ▶ I_____ o_____ using chopsticks, you can use a fork.

A 다음 ( ) 안에서 알맞은 것을 고르시오.

1 She will be back in (a little / a few) days.

2 There was (little / few) food in the fridge.

3 I have (a little / a few) time to talk with you.

4 I feel lonely because I have (little / few) friends.

B 우리말과 일치하도록 ( ) 안의 말을 이용하여 문장을 완성하시오.

1 나는 주머니에 동전 몇 개가 있다. (few, coin)
   ▶ I have _____ _____ _____ in my pocket.

2 그녀의 바람은 그 가수를 만나는 것이다. (meet, the singer)
   ▶ Her wish is _____ _____ _____ _____.

3 이 그림을 말리는 데 몇 시간이 걸릴 것이다. (few, hour)
   ▶ It will take _____ _____ _____ to dry this painting.

4 아침에 일찍 일어나는 것은 어렵다. (wake up)
   ▶ _____ is hard _____ _____ _____ early in the morning.

5 서랍장과 벽 사이에 공간이 약간 있다. (little, space)
   ▶ There is _____ _____ _____ between the drawer and the wall.

C 주어진 문장을 「it ~ to-v」의 형태로 바꾸어 쓰시오.

1 To know yourself is important.
   ▶ _____

2 To feel sleepy at night is natural.
   ▶ _____

3 To speak English fluently is hard.
   ▶ _____

A 우리말과 일치하도록 ( ) 안에 주어진 말을 바르게 배열하시오.

1 그곳은 영하 89도까지 추워질 수 있다. (as / as / cold / −89°C)

▶ It can get _____.

2 그는 세상에 새로운 관점을 제시했다. (gave / a new / the world / perspective)

▶ He _____.

3 모든 사막이 덥고 모래로 가득 찬 것은 아니다. (all / deserts/ not / are)

▶ _____ hot and full of sand.

4 이는 그 나라들이 '더 가치 있다'는 고정관념을 가중할 수 있다. (stereotypes / they / that / are)

▶ This can add to _____ "more valuable."

5 그의 목표는 사람들이 그의 나라에 대해 다르게 생각하도록 만드는 것이었다.

(to / people / make / think)

▶ His goal was _____ differently about his country.

6 그곳에는 물이 많이 없기 때문에, 사람들은 그곳이 매우 건조하다고 믿는 경향이 있다.

(they / have / since / much water / don't)

▶ _____, people tend to believe they are very

dry.

B 우리말과 일치하도록 ( ) 안의 말을 이용하여 문장을 완성하시오.

1 덥다는 것이 사막을 정의하지 않는다. (be, hot, not, define)

▶ _____ _____ _____ _____ a desert.

2 식물과 동물에게는 그곳에서 사는 것이 어렵다. (live, there, be)

▶ _____ _____ _____ hard for plants and animals.

3 그곳은 지구상에서 가장 더운 곳 중 하나이다. (one, of, hot, place)

▶ It is _____ _____ _____ _____ _____ on Earth.

4 익숙한 것을 새로운 방식으로 보는 것은 낯설게 느껴진다. (it, feel, strange, see)

▶ _____ _____ _____ _____ _____ familiar things in new

ways.

VOCABULARY TEST 1

반 / 이름:

[01–23] 다음 단어의 뜻을 쓰시오.

01 maintain _____

02 instrument _____

03 heatless _____

04 frozen _____

05 rare _____

06 retune _____

07 invent _____

08 impossible _____

09 metal _____

10 gather _____

11 glow _____

12 discover _____

13 performance _____

14 unique _____

15 freeze _____

16 ancient _____

17 including _____

18 pack _____

19 creativity _____

20 prevent _____

21 success _____

22 although _____

23 northern _____

[24–37] 다음 뜻을 지닌 단어를 쓰시오.

24 공연, 연주회 _____

25 쉽게 _____

26 녹다 _____

27 저렴한, 싼 _____

28 배; 운송하다 _____

29 무역, 교역 _____

30 냉장고 _____

31 저장[보관]하다 _____

32 자유로운; 무료의 _____

33 섬세한 주의를 요구하는 _____

34 청중, 관중 _____

35 인상적인, 인상 깊은 _____

36 줄; (악기의) 현 _____

37 연못 _____

[38–40] 다음 표현의 뜻을 쓰시오.

38 a variety of _____

39 take place _____

40 come up with _____

A 다음 영영 정의에 해당하는 단어를 고르시오.

> to produce a steady light that is not very bright

ⓐ retune   ⓑ glow   ⓒ pack   ⓓ prevent

B 다음 밑줄 친 단어와 비슷한 의미의 단어를 고르시오.

> It is <u>rare</u> to snow in April.

ⓐ expensive   ⓑ unusual   ⓒ possible   ⓓ common

C 다음 빈칸에 알맞은 단어를 보기에서 골라 쓰시오.

> 보기   gather   success   creativity   discover

1 His birthday party was a huge _____.

2 The team wants to _____ a new island.

3 Being a good artist requires a lot of _____.

4 A lot of people will _____ in front of city hall.

D 다음 우리말과 일치하도록 빈칸에 알맞은 말을 쓰시오.

1 그 화재는 이탈리아 식당에서 일어났다.

▶ The fire t_____ p_____ at the Italian restaurant.

2 그녀는 다양한 과일과 채소로 주스를 만들었다.

▶ She made juice with a v_____ o_____ fruits and vegetables.

3 그들은 새로운 주제를 생각해내기 위해 회의를 했다.

▶ They had a meeting to c_____ u_____ w_____ new topics.

A 다음 밑줄 친 to부정사(구)가 수식하는 것에 동그라미 하시오.

1 I don't have any secrets to hide.

2 Would you like something to drink?

3 He doesn't have clothes to wear tomorrow.

4 Anne has a lot of friends to invite to her party.

B 우리말과 일치하도록 ( ) 안의 말을 이용하여 문장을 완성하시오.

1 나는 택시를 탈 돈이 없다. (money, take)

▶ I have no ＿＿＿＿＿ ＿＿＿＿＿ ＿＿＿＿＿ a taxi.

2 그녀는 해야 할 숙제가 많이 있다. (homework, do)

▶ She has a lot of ＿＿＿＿＿ ＿＿＿＿＿ ＿＿＿＿＿.

3 나는 책 몇 권을 빌리기 위해 도서관에 갔다. (borrow, some books)

▶ I went to the library ＿＿＿＿＿ ＿＿＿＿＿ ＿＿＿＿＿ ＿＿＿＿＿.

4 나의 엄마는 식료품을 사기 위해 쇼핑을 갔다. (buy, some groceries)

▶ My mom went shopping ＿＿＿＿＿ ＿＿＿＿＿ ＿＿＿＿＿ ＿＿＿＿＿.

C 다음 문장을 우리말로 옮기시오.

1 I have something to tell you.

▶ ＿＿＿＿＿＿＿＿＿＿＿＿＿＿＿＿＿＿＿＿＿＿＿＿＿＿＿

2 He studied hard to enter university.

▶ ＿＿＿＿＿＿＿＿＿＿＿＿＿＿＿＿＿＿＿＿＿＿＿＿＿＿＿

3 She turned on the computer to check her email.

▶ ＿＿＿＿＿＿＿＿＿＿＿＿＿＿＿＿＿＿＿＿＿＿＿＿＿＿＿

4 Jeju Island is a good place to enjoy your vacation.

▶ ＿＿＿＿＿＿＿＿＿＿＿＿＿＿＿＿＿＿＿＿＿＿＿＿＿＿＿

A 우리말과 일치하도록 ( ) 안에 주어진 말을 바르게 배열하시오.

1 그는 바텐더들에게 사용해 볼 무료 얼음을 제공했다. (free / to / ice / try)
  ▶ He gave bartenders _____.

2 Tudor가 운송하려 했던 얼음의 대부분이 정말 녹아버렸다. (Tudor / to / ship / tried)
  ▶ Most of the ice _____ did melt.

3 악기들은 곡들 사이에 다시 조율되어야 한다. (retuned / must / be)
  ▶ The instruments _____ between songs.

4 그것들은 연주될 때마다 조금씩 녹기 때문이다. (each / played / are / they / time)
  ▶ This is because they melt a little _____.

5 공연은 관중이 너무 추워하는 것을 막기 위해 짧게 유지되어야 한다.

  (the audience / freezing / prevent / from)
  ▶ Performances must be kept short to _____.

B 우리말과 일치하도록 ( ) 안의 말을 이용하여 문장을 완성하시오.

1 악기들은 얼음으로 만들어진다. (be, make, of, ice)
  ▶ The instruments _____ _____ _____ _____.

2 그는 얼음을 저장하는 방법을 알아냈다. (store, the ice)
  ▶ He discovered a way _____ _____ _____ _____.

3 사람들은 얼음 음악 오케스트라를 듣기 위해 모인다. (gather, hear)
  ▶ People _____ _____ _____ the Ice Music orchestra.

4 요즘에, 얼음은 저렴하고 쉽게 구매될 수 있다. (can, buy)
  ▶ These days, ice is cheap and _____ _____ _____ easily.

5 그는 꽁꽁 언 겨울 연못에서 얼음을 가져다 세계의 더운 지역에 운송할 아이디어를 생각해냈다.

  (take, ice, from)
  ▶ He came up with the idea _____ _____ _____ _____ frozen

  winter ponds and ship it to hot parts of the world.

VOCABULARY TEST 1

반 / 이름:

[01-23] 다음 단어의 뜻을 쓰시오.

01 foolish

02 scream

03 brag

04 rower

05 pass

06 stick

07 risk

08 deed

09 row

10 amazingly

11 boast

12 talented

13 grab

14 protect

15 directly

16 single

17 cross

18 reveal

19 perform

20 halfway

21 yell

22 each

23 magically

[24-36] 다음 뜻을 지닌 단어를 쓰시오.

24 (시합 등에) 출전[참가]하다

25 (처)벌하다

26 영웅적인, 용감무쌍한

27 변장하다

28 (베 등을) 짜다, 엮다

29 여신

30 (대회 등의) 상대

31 잃어버리다; 패배하다

32 결국, 끝내

33 사건, 일; 종목, 경기

34 격노한, 몹시 화가 난

35 사진; 묘사

36 도전하다

[37-40] 다음 표현의 뜻을 쓰시오.

37 set a record

38 catch up with

39 take the lead

40 in front of

A 다음 영영 정의에 해당하는 단어를 고르시오.

> to change your appearance so that people cannot recognize you

ⓐ grab   ⓑ reveal   ⓒ cross   ⓓ disguise

B 다음 밑줄 친 단어와 비슷한 의미의 단어를 고르시오.

> Morris is only 10 years old, but he is a very <u>talented</u> musician.

ⓐ young   ⓑ busy   ⓒ gifted   ⓓ successful

C 다음 빈칸에 알맞은 단어를 보기에서 골라 쓰시오.

> 보기   deed   risk   punish   brag

1 You should try doing a good _____.

2 He wanted to _____ about his new sports car.

3 Stop smoking. You shouldn't _____ your health.

4 They _____ their children by not letting them watch TV.

D 다음 우리말과 일치하도록 빈칸에 알맞은 말을 쓰시오.

1 Jamie는 경주에서 선두에 서기 위해 노력했다.
   ▶ Jamie tried to t_____ t_____ l_____ in the race.

2 그 버스는 우리 학교 앞에서 멈춘다.
   ▶ The bus stops i_____ f_____ o_____ my school.

3 그는 그의 친구들을 따라잡기 위해 달리기 시작했다.
   ▶ He started to run to c_____ u_____ w_____ his friends.

A 다음 ( ) 안에서 알맞은 것을 고르시오.

1 She wants (to be / being) a famous singer.

2 He is planning (to study / studying) abroad.

3 We wish (to buy / buying) a new apartment.

4 Do you mind (to open / opening) the window?

B 다음 빈칸에 알맞은 단어를 보기 에서 골라 알맞은 형태로 쓰시오. (단, 한 번씩만 쓸 것)

보기	do	see	lose	look

1 We hope _____ you soon.

2 Mary kept _____ at her watch.

3 He finished _____ his homework.

4 Your dog needs _____ some weight.

C 우리말과 일치하도록 ( ) 안의 말을 이용하여 문장을 완성하시오.

1 너는 정크푸드를 먹는 것을 피해야 한다. (avoid, eat, junk food)
▶ You should _____ _____ _____ _____.

2 나의 아빠는 일 년 전에 담배 피우는 것을 끊었다. (give, up, smoke)
▶ My dad _____ _____ _____ a year ago.

3 그들은 일요일마다 영화를 보는 것을 즐긴다. (enjoy, watch, movies)
▶ They _____ _____ _____ every Sunday.

4 그녀는 다음 주까지 내 책을 돌려주기로 약속했다. (promise, return, my book)
▶ She _____ _____ _____ _____ _____ by next week.

A 우리말과 일치하도록 ( ) 안에 주어진 단어를 알맞게 배열하시오.

1 이 재능은 아테나가 당신에게 준 것인가요? (given / was / this talent)

▶ _____ to you by Athena?

2 아라크네의 묘사는 아테나를 격노하게 만들었다. (furious / made / Athena)

▶ Arachne's pictures _____.

3 아라크네와 아테나는 재빨리 베를 짜기 시작했다. (started / weave / to)

▶ Arachne and Athena quickly _____.

4 오리들이 지나간 뒤에, Pearce는 다시 노를 젓기 시작했다. (had / after / the ducks / passed)

▶ _____, Pearce began rowing again.

5 어떤 사람들은 삶에 있어서 승리보다 더 중요한 것이 있다는 것을 안다.

(are / there / more / that / important)

▶ Some people understand _____ things in life than

winning.

B 우리말과 일치하도록 ( ) 안의 말을 이용하여 문장을 완성하시오.

1 그는 경주에서 패배할 위험을 감수했다. (risk, lose, the race)

▶ He _____ _____ _____ _____.

2 그녀는 베를 짜는 데 매우 재능이 있었다. (very talented, at, weave)

▶ She was _____ _____ _____ _____.

3 그녀는 자기 자신을 늙은 여자로 변장하기로 결심했다. (decide, disguise, her)

▶ She _____ _____ _____ _____ as an old woman.

4 그의 상대편은 계속 노를 저었고 선두에 섰다. (keep, row, and, take)

▶ His opponent _____ _____ _____ _____ the lead.

5 1928년 올림픽에서, 그는 1인 조정 경기 종목에 출전 중이었다. (he, be, compete)

▶ In the 1928 Olympics, _____ _____ _____ in the single sculls event.

VOCABULARY TEST 1

반 / 이름:

[01-23] 다음 단어의 뜻을 쓰시오.

01 route _____

02 within _____

03 lay _____

04 amazing _____

05 fully _____

06 wild _____

07 eel _____

08 depth _____

09 gender _____

10 active _____

11 major _____

12 flat _____

13 crew _____

14 explore _____

15 surroundings _____

16 prove _____

17 surprisingly _____

18 untrue _____

19 beneath _____

20 ocean _____

21 calmness _____

22 enormous _____

23 produce _____

[24-36] 다음 뜻을 지닌 단어를 쓰시오.

24 안타깝게도, 불행히도 _____

25 셀 수 없이 많은 _____

26 외형, 모습 _____

27 수컷 _____

28 생물, 생명체 _____

29 낯선, 익숙하지 않은 _____

30 암컷 _____

31 항해, 여행 _____

32 발견 _____

33 흔들리다 _____

34 항해사, 조종사 _____

35 (색 등이) 밝은 _____

36 다 자란, 성인의 _____

[37-40] 다음 표현의 뜻을 쓰시오.

37 be born _____

38 come upon _____

39 derived from _____

40 up to _____

A 다음 영영 정의에 해당하는 단어를 고르시오.

> the way that somebody or something looks on the outside

ⓐ calmness   ⓑ route   ⓒ appearance   ⓓ depth

B 다음 밑줄 친 단어와 반대 의미의 단어를 고르시오.

> I'd like to use that <u>bright</u> orange crayon.

ⓐ rough   ⓑ dark   ⓒ minor   ⓓ entire

C 다음 빈칸에 알맞은 단어를 보기에서 골라 쓰시오.

> 보기   lay   prove   voyage   discovery

1 They started their _____ to Australia.

2 The scientist reported his new _____.

3 These chickens _____ eggs every morning.

4 This evidence will _____ that she did nothing wrong.

D 다음 우리말과 일치하도록 빈칸에 알맞은 말을 쓰시오.

1 물이 내 무릎까지 차올랐다.
   ▶ The water came u_____ t_____ my knees.

2 그는 지하에서 지도를 우연히 발견했다.
   ▶ He c_____ u_____ a map in the basement.

3 수많은 영단어들은 라틴어에서 유래되었다.
   ▶ So many English words were d_____ f_____ Latin.

A 다음 ( ) 안에서 알맞은 것을 고르시오.

1 Is this notebook yours (but / or) his?

2 I had coffee (and / but) doughnuts for breakfast.

3 I often eat too much (before / when) I feel very hungry.

4 (After / Before) they get home, they always lay on their couch.

B 다음 빈칸에 알맞은 단어를 보기에서 골라 쓰시오. (단, 한 번씩만 쓸 것)

보기	and	but	when	before

1 I was confused _____ I saw the exam.

2 I already had dinner, _____ I'm still hungry.

3 Melt the butter _____ you put it in the bowl.

4 There are lots of buses _____ taxis on the road.

C 우리말과 일치하도록 ( ) 안의 말을 이용하여 문장을 완성하시오.

1 나는 밀가루와 우유를 살 것이다. (flour, milk)

▶ I'll buy some _____ _____ _____.

2 이 샌드위치는 저렴하지만 맛있다. (cheap, tasty)

▶ This sandwich is _____ _____ _____.

3 나는 어렸을 때, 부산에 살았다. (I, was, young)

▶ _____ _____ _____ _____, I lived in Busan.

4 네가 저녁을 먹기 전에, 숙제를 먼저 끝내라. (you, have, dinner)

▶ _____ _____ _____ _____, finish your homework first.

반 / 이름:

A 우리말과 일치하도록 ( ) 안에 주어진 말을 바르게 배열하시오.

1 그것은 알을 낳은 뒤 약 한 달 이내에 죽는다. (lays / it / eggs / after)
   ▶ It dies within about a month _____.

2 야생에서 노란색 리본 장어를 발견하는 것은 쉽지 않다. (to / is / not easy / it / find)
   ▶ _____ yellow ribbon eels in the wild.

3 그것이 노란색으로 바뀌면, 암컷이 되고 알을 낳을 수 있다! (it / yellow / turns / when)
   ▶ _____, it becomes female and can lay eggs!

4 그의 작은 무리의 배들은 낯선 바다를 우연히 발견했다. (an unfamiliar / upon / came / ocean)
   ▶ His small group of ships _____.

5 그는 향료 제도가 매우 가까이에 있다고 믿었지만, 그것은 사실이 아닌 것으로 판명 났다.
   (would / untrue / prove / that)
   ▶ He believed the Spice Islands were very near, but _____.

B 우리말과 일치하도록 ( ) 안의 말을 이용하여 문장을 완성하시오.

1 우리는 여전히 이 거대한 바다를 많이 탐험하지 못했다. (have, explore)
   ▶ We still _____ _____ much of this enormous ocean.

2 그것이 점점 더 커지면서, 그것의 몸통은 밝은 파란색으로 바뀐다. (as, it, get, big)
   ▶ _____ _____ _____ _____, its body turns bright blue.

3 이것은 꼭 물속에서 흔들리는 화려한 리본처럼 보인다. (wave, in, the water)
   ▶ It looks just like a colorful ribbon _____ _____ _____ _____.

4 태평양은 지구의 오대양 중 가장 깊고 크다. (deep, and, large)
   ▶ The Pacific Ocean is _____ _____ _____ _____ of the five
   major oceans on Earth.

5 그 이름 자체는 16세기에 포르투갈 항해사 Ferdinand Magellan에 의해 지어졌다. (be, give, by)
   ▶ The name itself _____ _____ _____ Portuguese navigator Ferdinand
   Magellan in the 16th century.

UNIT 12 | Environment

VOCABULARY TEST 1

반 / 이름:

[01-22] 다음 단어의 뜻을 쓰시오.

01 pollution _____

02 return _____

03 half _____

04 reverse _____

05 ocean _____

06 spread _____

07 creativity _____

08 reduce _____

09 surface _____

10 form _____

11 human _____

12 result _____

13 attack _____

14 beach _____

15 wall _____

16 survive _____

17 hatch _____

18 possible _____

19 normally _____

20 harmful _____

21 material _____

22 recently _____

[23-35] 다음 뜻을 지닌 단어를 쓰시오.

23 포식 동물, 포식자 _____

24 대조, 차이 _____

25 도달하다 _____

26 마지막의, 마지막 남은 _____

27 성체; 다 자란 _____

28 추세, 동향 _____

29 (알·새끼를) 낳다 _____

30 피하다 _____

31 암컷의 _____

32 필요하다, 요구하다 _____

33 일시적인, 임시의 _____

34 직면하다 _____

35 돌고래 _____

[36-40] 다음 표현의 뜻을 쓰시오.

36 in danger _____

37 out of _____

38 make one's way to _____

39 clean away _____

40 known as _____

VOCABULARY TEST 2

A 다음 영영 정의에 해당하는 단어를 고르시오.

> the process of making air, water, or soil dirty

ⓐ pollution　　　　ⓑ ocean　　　　ⓒ material　　　　ⓓ creativity

B 다음 밑줄 친 단어와 반대 의미의 단어를 고르시오.

> This medicine will help <u>reduce</u> the fever.

ⓐ stop　　　　ⓑ lower　　　　ⓒ increase　　　　ⓓ produce

C 다음 빈칸에 알맞은 단어를 보기에서 골라 쓰시오.

> 보기　　last　　　hatch　　　reach　　　result

1 The eggs are just about to _____.

2 He died as a _____ of his injuries.

3 You can have the _____ piece of cake.

4 They hoped to _____ the camp before dark.

D 다음 우리말과 일치하도록 빈칸에 알맞은 말을 쓰시오.

1 Pablo는 유명한 예술가로 알려져 있다.
  ▶ Pablo is k_____ a_____ a famous artist.

2 북극곰은 멸종할 위험에 처해 있다.
  ▶ Polar bears are i_____ d_____ of going extinct.

3 그는 강당의 앞으로 나아갔다.
  ▶ He m_____ his w_____ t_____ the front of the auditorium.

Reading Inside Starter | **47**

A 다음 ( ) 안에서 알맞은 것을 고르시오.

1 I won't go to the soccer game (if / because) it rains later.

2 (That / Because) I am sick, I cannot play sports anymore.

3 I have learned (if / that) math can be a very difficult subject.

4 The problem is (that / because) I don't have enough money.

B 보기에서 알맞은 단어를 골라 다음 문장의 밑줄 친 부분을 바르게 고치시오. (중복 사용 가능)

> 보기   if   because   that

1 Everyone knows <u>because</u> she did her best.   _____

2 His hope is <u>because</u> he will become a doctor.   _____

3 Jack had a stomachache <u>that</u> he ate too much.   _____

4 Raise your hand <u>because</u> you have any questions.   _____

C 다음 문장을 우리말로 옮기시오.

1 If it snows a lot, the event will be canceled.

   ▶ _____

2 She was very tired because she worked too hard.

   ▶ _____

3 His opinion is that everyone should participate in the game.

   ▶ _____

4 If you don't wake up early tomorrow, you will be late for school.

   ▶ _____

A 우리말과 일치하도록 ( ) 안에 주어진 말을 바르게 배열하시오.

1 그들은 바다를 향해 나아가야 한다. (their / must / way / make)

  ▶ They _____ to the ocean.

2 리버스 그라피티는 광고의 한 유형으로 사용되고 있다. (as / used / has / been)

  ▶ Reverse graffiti _____ a form of advertising.

3 포스터와 전단 같은 광고는 많은 재료를 사용한다. (as / posters / such / leaflets / and)

  ▶ Advertisements _____ use lots of materials.

4 그들은 다른 동물들에 의해 공격받고, 그들의 절반은 잡아먹힌다. (them / eaten / of / are / half)

  ▶ They are attacked by other animals, and _____.

5 그것들은 살아남은 다 자란 바다거북의 수를 고작 두 마리로 줄여 버린다.

  (surviving / number / of / the)

  ▶ They reduce _____ adult sea turtles to just two.

B 우리말과 일치하도록 ( ) 안의 말을 이용하여 문장을 완성하시오.

1 바다거북에게 생존은 항상 어려웠다. (have, always, be, difficult)

  ▶ Survival _____ _____ _____ _____ for sea turtles.

2 인간이 그 문제를 훨씬 더 악화시키고 있다. (make, the problem, much, bad)

  ▶ Humans are _____ _____ _____ _____ _____.

3 무언가를 지움으로써 그라피티를 만들어 내는 것이 가능하다. (possible, create, graffiti)

  ▶ It's _____ _____ _____ _____ by erasing something.

4 이미지는 깨끗한 부분과 더러운 부분 간의 대조에 의해 만들어진다. (make, by)

  ▶ Images _____ _____ _____ the contrast between the clean part and
  the dirty part.

5 리버스 그라피티는, 깨끗한 그라피티라고도 알려져 있으며, 전통적인 그라피티에 대한 발상을 뒤집는다.

  (know, as, clean graffiti)

  ▶ Reverse graffiti, also _____ _____ _____ _____, reverses the
  idea of traditional graffiti.

READING
Inside

workbook

A 4-level curriculum
integration reading course

· **A thematic reading program that integrates with school curriculum**
중등 교육과정이 지향하는 문이과 통합 및 타교과 연계 반영한 독해서

· **Informative content with well-designed comprehension questions**
정보성 있는 지문과 질 높은 다양한 유형의 문항 그리고 서술형 평가도 대비

· **Grammar points directly related to the *Grammar Inside* series**
베스트셀러 Grammar Inside와 직접적으로 연계된 문법 항목 및 문항 제공

· **Exercises with useful, essential, and academic vocabulary**
중등 필수 어휘 학습 코너 제공

· **A workbook for more vocabulary, grammar, and reading exercises**
풍부한 양의 어휘, 문법, 그리고 쓰기 추가 문제 등을 수록한 워크북

Level	Grade	Words Limit
Reading Inside Starter	**Low-Intermediate**	**140-160**
Reading Inside Level 1	Intermediate	160-180
Reading Inside Level 2	Intermediate	180-200
Reading Inside Level 3	Low-Advanced	200-220